Association Law Update:

The 2009 Supplement to

Association Law Handbook,

4th Edition

Jerald A. Jacobs

The author has worked diligently to ensure that all information in this book is accurate as of the time of publication and consistent with standards of good practice in the general management community. As research and practice advance, however, standards may change. For this reason it is recommended that readers evaluate the applicability of any recommendations in light of particular situations and changing standards.

ASAE & The Center for Association Leadership
1575 I Street, NW
Washington, DC 20005-1103
Phone: (202) 626-2723; (888) 950-2723 outside the metropolitan Washington, DC, area
Fax: (202) 220-6439
E-mail: books@asaecenter.org
We connect great ideas and great people to inspire leadership and achievement in the association community.

Keith C. Skillman, CAE, Vice President, Publications, ASAE & The Center for Association Leadership
Baron Williams, CAE, Director of Book Publishing, ASAE & The Center for Association Leadership

Cover design by Beth Lower, Art Director, ASAE & The Center for Association Leadership

This book is available at a special discount when ordered in bulk quantities. For information, contact the ASAE Member Service Center at (202) 371-0940.
A complete catalog of titles is available on the ASAE & The Center for Association Leadership website at www.asaecenter.org.

ISBN-13: 978-0-88034-312-1
ISBN-10: 0-88034-312-5

Printed in the United States of America.

10 9 8 7 6 5 4 3 2 1

About the Author

Jerald A. Jacobs is an attorney in Washington, D.C., who focuses on counseling and advocacy for business, professional, social welfare, philanthropic, and other nonprofit organizations. He serves as General Counsel to ASAE, the major national association of nonprofit organization executive leadership, and its interdependent education and research affiliate, The Center for Association Leadership. He has taught nonprofit organization law at graduate law and business schools, he has been recognized by the American Bar Association for his work in the nonprofit organization field, and he has advised the governments of the European Union and the People's Republic of China on their laws for nongovernmental organizations.

Contents

Introduction

As law and policy affecting associations evolves, my goal and that of ASAE and The Center for Association Leadership is to inform you of the changes in the accessible, practical format used in each edition of *Association Law Handbook*. That goal informed the conception and development of this 2009 supplement, which is intended for use in conjunction with *Association Law Handbook, 4th Edition*. With both the comprehensive book and this supplement, you will have at your disposal the complete picture of the most important association and nonprofit legal and policy developments.

Notable developments since 2007, when *Association Law Handbook* was last published, include the following:

- The Internal Revenue Service issued its first major revision in 30 years to the annual informational return filed by tax-exempt organizations, Form 990 (2008), adding unprecedented disclosure and governance provisions at the urging of Congress.

- Congress passed the Honest Leadership and Open Government Act, expanding federal lobbying reporting requirements and prohibiting the provision by lobbyists of honoraria, gifts, and travel to members and employees of Congress.

- The Federal Trade Commission entered into an antitrust settlement with a national trade association in which the FTC challenged mere price discussions at the association's events even in the absence of conventional anticompetitive conduct.

These changes, along with less dramatic but still important developments, are covered in this supplement. The changes were also a catalyst for the creation of several new model forms, such as the *Basic Form 990 Governance Policies/Procedures* document, which is intended to assist associations with a quick and easy policy package for Form 990 compliance. Overall, five new model forms have been added both in print and on the CD-ROM to complement the 25 sample or model forms included in the 4th Edition.

The 2007 4th Edition of the book, with almost 600 pages, inevitably contained the odd unclear statement or outright error; all of those that have come to the author's attention also have been addressed, beginning on page XXX. The author would be most grateful if readers who find others will advise about them.

This 2009 supplement is a collaborative effort; a number of distinguished professionals assisted in making it as comprehensive, accurate, practical, and timely as possible. Fred Lowell and Emily Barrett worked tirelessly to revise the lobbying and political law chapters, reflecting the many recent changes in these areas. Jeff Glassie, Audra Heagney, and Megan Thorsen helped update existing chapters, write new ones, and produce additional model documents for this Supplement. The author is extremely grateful to these colleagues/friends for their invaluable and expert assistance.

The first edition of *Association Law Handbook* appeared in 1981. Nonprofit organizations in the United States have advanced dramatically since then, becoming larger, more sophisticated, better managed, and increasingly creative and responsive to the needs of members, donors, and other constituents. The author sincerely hopes that this book has assisted in even a small way in helping "Associations Advance America."

Jerald A. Jacobs
Washington, D.C.
July 2009

New Chapters

Chapter 39A
Charitable Solicitation

Any tax-exempt organization that engages in solicitation of charitable contributions, also known as charitable fund-raising or development, must comply with federal and state laws, regulations, and requirements pertaining to that solicitation. Federal and state laws and regulations specify permitted methods of solicitation, disclosure requirements, documentation obligations, tax deductibility, and related provisions. The federal laws are uniform in applying to all charitable organizations soliciting of contributions. In contrast, state laws are usually complex and lacking in uniformity; states differ in both their requirements and their enforcement. While all organizations that engage in charitable solicitation are subject to federal provisions, an organization is subject to state provisions only if physically present in the state or soliciting contributions in the state. States often require such an organization to register with the state, as well as to provide annual financial reports detailing charitable solicitation activity.

Charitable solicitation provisions primarily apply to conventional charitable organizations and individuals who engage in charitable fund-raising for those organizations. However, there are circumstances in which charitable solicitation laws apply to other categories of tax-exempt organizations. The definition of "charitable organizations" in the context of state charitable solicitation laws can be broader than might be expected. Federal regulations, of course, apply to charitable organizations, those exempt under Section 501(c)(3) of the Internal Revenue Code, but the regulations may also apply to organizations tax exempt in other categories but unable to attract deductible contributions, such as social welfare or "cause" organizations under Section 501(c)(4) of the Code. And there are other categories of tax-exempt organizations eligible to receive deductible contributions but not regarded as charitable, such as veterans groups under Section 501(c)(19) of the Code. All of these can be subject to charitable solicitation provisions.

The solicitation of charitable contributions can be undertaken in a variety of ways, and donors can contribute in a variety of ways. Charitable organizations and their employees or volunteers might solicit contributions on behalf of the organizations; alternatively, they might engage professional fund-raisers to do so. The requirements under both federal and state laws may encompass these various modes. So organizations engaging in any kind of charitable solicitation, fund-raising, or development activity should ensure that they are in compliance.

Summary

- Charitable solicitation may take many forms. Contributions may be solicited by mail, by telephone, in person, or online, and may be conducted through a variety of programs.

- ◆ A charitable organization may solicit contributions through annual giving programs, which generally focus on recruiting new donors and maintaining prior donors; these programs are used to ensure the continuing general financial success of the organization.

- ◆ An organization may solicit contributions for specific special projects, which are often funded by major gifts from individuals; grants from government agencies, foundations, or corporations; or capital campaigns.

- ◆ Finally, organizations may solicit funds for gift planning, or rather, gifts that are made in the present and are to be realized by the organization in the future, such as a bequest in a will.

- An organization must also take into consideration the individual(s) that will be soliciting contributions on behalf of the organization, as legislation and regulations set forth guidelines for the relationship between organizations and the individuals who solicit funds on their behalf.

  - ◆ An organization may have one or more fund-raising or development executive, who might be a full time salaried employee of the organization. The federal and state provisions in this instance tend to regulate the organization and not its employees.

  - ◆ Alternatively, an organization may hire a fund-raising consultant, which may be an individual or firm providing consultation on the conduct of fund-raising. Many state regulations require these consultants to register with the state authorities, file copies of contracts for service, and be bonded if the consultants are required to handle charitable contributions.

  - ◆ Finally, an organization may engage a professional solicitor on a fee basis to create and conduct a complete fund-raising program on behalf of the organization. The regulations surrounding a professional solicitor are the most stringent.

- Although there is no federal charitable solicitation law, as such, the federal government regulates charitable solicitation through several regulatory schemes. For example, Internal Revenue provisions require that charitable organizations assist in ensuring that contributions are not considered by the donors to be fully tax deductible when they are only partially tax deductible.

- A charitable contribution where the donor receives value in return is tax deductible by the donor only to the extent that it exceeds the value received by the donor. It is the obligation of the charitable organization to inform donors of this distinction between deductible and nondeductible donations or portions of donations. Nondeductible contributions include those where an event admission, a meal, or award merchandise is received in return.

◆ In the case of a fund-raising event in which something of value is provided to the donor, such as food or entertainment, the charity must determine the fair market value of what is provided and notify the donor that only the amount of the payment in excess of that value is tax deductible by the donor as a charitable gift. This nondeductible portion of a payment must be clearly stated on any sort of evidence of payment provided to the donor.

◆ Some benefits received in connection with a payment to a charitable organization may be considered to have insubstantial fair market value. In this context, payment is fully deductible as a charitable gift if two requirements are met. The first requirement is that the payment occurs in the context of a fund-raising campaign in which the charity informs donors of the amounts of their gifts considered tax-deductible contributions. The second requirement is that either: (1) the fair market value of all of the benefits received in connection with the contribution is not more than the lesser of 2 percent of the contribution or $95.00; or (2) the contribution is $47.50 or more, and the only benefits received in connection with the contribution are token items bearing the organization's name or logo. These amounts were adjusted for inflation as of 2008. Token items include the likes of bookmarks, calendars, key chains, mugs, posters, etc. The costs of all of the benefits received by a donor must in the aggregate be within the statutory limits established for a low-cost article, which is an article with a cost no more than $9.50.

• In general, the Internal Revenue Code provides that a charitable contribution may be deducted by a donor only if verified.

◆ Gifts of $250 or more are to be substantiated by a contemporaneous written acknowledgment by the charity that meets certain requirements. This acknowledgment must include: a description (but not value) of any property contributed; a statement as to whether the organization provided any goods or services in consideration for the donated property; and a description and good faith estimate of the value of any such goods or services provided by the organization.

◆ If a charitable organization receives a quid pro quo contribution in excess of $75, the organization must provide a written statement that informs the donor that the amount of the contribution that is deductible for federal income tax purposes is limited to the excess of the amount of any money, and the value of any property other than money, contributed by the donor over the value of goods and services provided by the organization, and provide the donor with a good faith estimate of the value of those goods or services provided by the organization.

♦ This does not include any payment made to an organization, organized exclusively for religious purposes, in return for which the taxpayer receives solely intangible religious benefit that generally is not sold in a commercial transaction outside the donative context.

♦ If an organization fails to meet the disclosure requirements set forth in the Internal Revenue Code, the organization must pay a penalty of $10 for each contribution in respect of which the organization fails to make the required disclosure, except that the total penalty imposed with respect to a particular fund-raising event or mailing should not exceed $5,000. No penalty is imposed if it is shown that a failure is due to reasonable cause.

• The Internal Revenue Code sets forth provisions which prevent noncharitable tax-exempt organizations from engaging in public fund-raising activities under circumstances in which donors are likely to assume that the contributions are tax deductible as charitable gifts, when in fact they are not. Every fund-raising solicitation by, or on behalf of, a noncharitable tax-exempt organization must contain an express statement in a conspicuous and easily recognizable format that contributions or gifts to the organization are not deductible as charitable contributions for federal income tax purposes.

♦ There are several exceptions to this requirement. It does not apply to any organization that has gross receipts less than $100,000 for the taxable year. It also does not apply to any letter or telephone call that is not part of a fund-raising campaign soliciting more than ten persons during the calendar year. An exception is also made if all of the parties being solicited are tax-exempt organizations since these organizations are not liable for the payment of taxes and charitable contribution deductions do not apply to them.

♦ If an organization makes a solicitation to which these disclosure requirements apply and the solicitation does not comply, the Internal Revenue Service will evaluate all the facts and circumstances to determine whether the solicitation contained an express statement that the contributions are not deductible as charitable contributions.

♦ A good faith effort to comply with the disclosure requirements will be an important factor in the evaluation of the facts and circumstances.

The failure to include the required disclosure could result in a penalty of $1,000 for each day on which such a failure occurs, up to a maximum annual penalty of $10,000. For cases in which the failure to make the disclosure is found to be due to intentional disregard of the law, the $10,000 per year limitation on the penalty does not apply and more severe penalties based on up to 50 percent of the aggregate cost of the solicitations is applicable.

- In addition to federal requirements, charitable organizations must comply with the state solicitation laws in states in which the organizations solicit contributions. It is sometimes difficult to determine whether solicitation has been directed at a particular state. A letter, phone call, or newspaper ad requesting financial support from a state's residents is enough to trigger required compliance with a state's solicitation law. If an organization has purposefully directed a charitable solicitation to a resident of the state, the state may exercise jurisdiction.

- Despite the non-uniformity amongst the different state statutes, 35 states have adopted some form of a standard state charitable solicitation act. Several basic common features shared by these statutes are set forth here; although, any organization soliciting funds in a state must consult that state's specific code of regulations to determine the requirements that must be met.

  - Almost all state charitable solicitation acts require that the organization register with, or receive approval from, the state prior to engaging in charitable solicitation within the state. This registration or permission is generally made to the office of the secretary of state or to the attorney general; and information required to be submitted is generally mandated by statute.

  - In most state statutes, the state maintains the authority to withdraw or revoke the authorization to solicit funds in the state in the event that the organization has violated a provision of the state's charitable solicitation law.

  - Most state acts require annual reporting with the appropriate governmental agency; this filing will generally serve as an informational report as well as an update of the organization's registration with the state. Although each state's reporting requirements are different, most generally require reporting regarding the amount of contributions obtained by the organization, the percentage of such amounts that will be devoted to charitable activities and the percentage devoted to fund-raising costs, identification of professional fund-raisers, and the amounts disbursed to particular categories.

◆ States often provide exemptions from reporting requirements; in some states such exemption is express, and in others organizations must apply for exemption. Churches and other religious organizations, educational institutions, and organizations that solicit only from their memberships are often exempt from such requirements.

◆ Generally, there are separate registration requirements for professional fund-raisers and professional solicitors. A professional fund-raiser must register with the state on an individual basis before the fund-raiser may act on behalf of an organization. Additionally, many states require annual reporting and/or registration by the fund-raiser.

◆ Although statutes limiting the amount of money that may be expended by an organization on fund-raising costs have been largely repealed, several state statutes do require disclosure of the amounts or percentages of the contributions retained by professional fund-raisers or solicitors and those passed on to the organization.

◆ Enforcement of the state's charitable solicitation provisions is generally managed by the state's attorney general. Numerous penalties may be levied in the event of violation of the state's laws. Among these are revocation, cancellation or denial of registration, investigations by government officials, fines and penalties, and injunctive action; some states even permit the levying of criminal penalties.

• Generally, compliance reporting under state solicitation laws is divided into two pieces: registration and annual financial reporting. Each state that regulates charitable solicitation has its own registration form; in response to this, the Unified Registration Statement ("URS") has been created. The URS may be used to fulfill the registration requirements in each state; however, it cannot be used to fulfill annual financial reporting requirements in many states. The URS was organized by the National Association of State Charities Officials and the National Association of Attorneys General, and it aims to standardize and simplify compliance under the states' solicitation laws. The URS is meant to serve as an alternative to filing all of the respective registration forms produced by each of the cooperating states. However, a number of states require additional forms and/or information to be provided.

Chapter 39A Resources

Books
Hopkins. *The Law of Fund-raising,* 2d ed. John Wiley, 1996.

Statutes and Regulations
Internal Revenue Code of 1986, as amended, 26 U.S.C. Section 170(a)(1).
Internal Revenue Code of 1986, as amended, 26 U.S.C. Section 170(f)(8).
Internal Revenue Code of 1986, as amended, 26 U.S.C. Section 6113.
Internal Revenue Code of 1986, as amended, 26 U.S.C. Section 6115(a).
Internal Revenue Code of 1986, as amended, 26 U.S.C. Section 6710.
Internal Revenue Code of 1986, as amended, 26 U.S.C. Section 6714.

Cases
United States v. American Bar Endowment, 477 U.S. 105, 116–117 (1986). "A payment of money generally cannot constitute a charitable contribution if the contributor expects a substantial benefit in return."
Revenue Ruling 67-246, 1967-2 CB 104. A payment to a charitable organization is not a gift if the donor receives something of approximately equal value in return.
Revenue Procedure 2008-66, 2008-45 IRB 1107, (Oct. 16, 2008).
Internal Revenue Notice 88-120, 1988-2 CB 454.

Chapter 68
Certification of Professionals

A basic purpose of virtually every individual membership organization is to improve the level of services provided within the profession or field represented by the organization. The goal of promoting professional competence is a worthy one that benefits members of the field itself as well as members of the public who deal with them.

Associations can promote individual competence in many ways: presenting informative meetings and education programs, publishing literature of interest to practitioners, sponsoring research in areas of concern to the field, and promulgating and enforcing codes of acceptable conduct.

One further avenue for individual membership organizations to improve their members' competence is certification. Certification by nonprofit nongovernmental organizations or by affiliated boards should be distinguished from occupational licensing, which is performed by state governments rather than by private organizations. State licensing of individuals exists as a legal condition for practicing an occupation, or utilizing a professional title, rather than as a voluntary measure of competence.

Nongovernmental certification of individuals has become a common activity. It is the rare professional society today that has not organized or does not operate, support, or sponsor a certification program. Through these activities a profession or field takes responsibility for prescribing educational and ethical qualifications for candidates for certification, administering competitive examinations, and awarding some signs of qualification to the successful. In addition, the certifying body retains jurisdiction to revoke certification from an individual who ceases to meet required minimum qualifications.

For the certified individual, the hallmark provides prestige, recognition, and possibly increased earning power. Equally important, certification enables the public (as well as government and private third-party payers for professional services) to distinguish between those that have attained some qualifying level of competency from those that have not.

In short, professional certification programs protect the public by helping individuals readily identify competent people, and simultaneously aid the profession or field by encouraging and recognizing individual competency or achievement.

Despite the ubiquitous benefits provided by private certification, certain aspects of such programs have at times come under legal attack. The Federal Trade Commission (FTC) and the Department of Justice have pursued alleged illegal practices in this field. In addition, occasionally private suits have arisen against certification programs, usually brought by those who have been excluded from qualification.

The next two chapters present some legal background and guidance for nonprofit nongovernmental certification programs based on the decisions and opinions expressed in government and private challenges to the programs, as well as other best practice considerations. This chapter mainly addresses certification generally; the next chapter mainly addresses legal issues in administration of certification programs.

Summary

- Professional certification programs operated, supported, or sponsored by nonprofit membership organizations typically rely on a combination of criteria, standards, or principles as factors that may help the profession and the public distinguish between individuals who are more likely to be competent than others. The combination usually includes education, experience, and testing. No program can guarantee the competence of individuals; too many factors besides certification determine the quality of profession services. And those providing or holding certification should guard against assuming or asserting that noncertified individuals are not competent or even less competent than those that are certified. The most that can be said is that certified individuals have taken the initiative to measure their own qualifications against the profession's consensus criteria, standards, or principles of competence; other individuals have not. Although professional certification therefore has inherent limitations—it cannot guarantee competence—it is nevertheless widely used by the public, by employers, by reimburses or by others as a measure of competence. It is therefore often greatly desired by those who aspire to advance and improve in a profession. Not surprisingly, those who have been excluded from eligibility for certification, or who have tried and failed to achieve it, may be inclined to bring legal attacks against the professional certification programs that they perceive as restraining or even damaging their professional prerogatives. It is not an exaggeration to say that professional certification is a "lightning rod" for legal complaints, charges, claims, and even lawsuits.

- Nongovernmental professional certification programs are ultimately quasi-public undertakings. They assume essential, if not primary, roles on behalf of the public rather than on behalf of the individuals in the professions or fields they serve. A review of all of the court cases and federal agency pronouncements on professional certification leads to an inescapable conclusion that the programs most likely to be endorsed, or at least not criticized or penalized, in those precedents are the ones where the public interest has been placed uppermost. If instead interests of professional fees or income, exclusion, or inhibition of individuals from practice, enhancement of related professional societies, or other goals inconsistent with the quasi-public role of certification are seen by objective reviewers as permeating or dominating decision-making, adverse rulings were likely to result.

• A Supreme Court case concerning a minimum fee schedule for professional legal services held that activities of the "learned professions" are subject to review under the antitrust laws as trade or commerce. However, the Court did reserve some semblance of a distinction for professions by saying that it would be "unrealistic to view the practice of professions as interchangeable with other business activities, and automatically apply to the professions antitrust concepts which originated in other areas" *(Goldfarb v. Virginia State Bar)*.

• The Supreme Court held that an engineer association's ban on competitive bidding was an antitrust violation, regardless of the ban's reasonableness. An important reference to certification appears in this decision in a concurring opinion stating that the Court might be willing to grant some extra margin under the antitrust laws and analyze the reasonableness of, as an example, "a medical association's prescription of standards of minimum competence for licensing or certification." Although not providing an antitrust exemption for professional certification, it is possible that the Court might view that activity with some additional leniency *(National Society of Professional Engineers v. United States)*.

• The Department of Justice has given its advice to an association on a proposed professional certification program. An audio-visual association proposed to confer the title of "Certified Media Specialist" on qualifying individual professionals. In its advice to the association indicating there would be no antitrust challenge, the Department of Justice relied on several aspects of the proposed program as important:

  ◆ Initial certification would be granted without examinations on the basis of successful completion of certain association-sponsored courses or on the basis of a certain number of years of professional experience.

  ◆ Recertification would be granted after a certain number of years if additional courses were taken.

  ◆ Certification, recertification, and courses would be open to members and nonmembers alike (although fees for nonmembers could be higher to reflect members' support of the activities through their payment of dues).

- ◆ De-certification would result only from failure to maintain certified status, not for ethical reasons.

- ◆ The association would not discourage anyone from dealing with uncertified individuals and would not overtly recommend certified individuals to customers or suppliers.

- The FTC once refused to issue an advisory opinion approving a proposed plan by an association of moving consultants to certify "professional moving consultants," who were described as estimators and salespeople for moving services. FTC claimed that:

  - ◆ The purposes of the program were too closely related to pricing of moving services.

  - ◆ Standards for refusing or revoking certification were too vague.

  - ◆ There were sufficient, less restrictive alternative methods for obtaining certification already available.

- Subsequently, FTC also refused to issue an advisory opinion approving a certification program for pedorthics professionals. While noting that "certification programs can be helpful to consumers by informing them that practitioners (and establishments) meet meaningful levels of occupational competency," the Commission cited what it considered several failings in the proposed plan:

  - ◆ The required qualifications for applicants were too indefinite.

  - ◆ There was no process for appealing adverse decisions to a body other than the credentialing group itself.

  - ◆ Certified professionals would be subject to "unreasonable" ethical restrictions, such as a tacit ban on advertising.

- Legal precedent for the adequacy of policies and procedures used in professional certification programs also can be found in non-government cases brought against certification bodies by individuals denied certification.

- Two state cases are important because they illustrate issues of denial of certification to health care professionals. In one case, the denial was upheld; in the other, it was overturned.

  - ◆ In the case upholding denial, admission to a defendant psychological association (which was effectively a certification process) was not a prerequisite for employment as a professional psychologist because there already existed a separate state occupational licensing program *(Salter v. New York State Psychological Ass'n)*.

  - ◆ In the case overturning a denial, admission to a defendant medical society (again, effectively a certification process) was the prerequisite for employment as a physician, because without society membership a physician could not use local hospital facilities *(Falcone v. Middlesex County Medical Soc'y)*.

• The lesson is that courts will look closely at, and overturn more readily, those decisions by certification bodies where the certification is a prerequisite for employment.

• In the context of professional certification, the question often arises as to whether certification equates with competence. The failure to accurately describe the scope of certification could ultimately lead to legal liability for a certification board or sponsoring association. Conclusions about the competence of individual professionals cannot be reached based on certification status alone and, therefore, it is important to be cautious about claims made or language used in describing related programs. A number of issues lead to the conclusion that it is unwise to equate competency exclusively with professional certification.

  ◆ Certification cannot guarantee or ensure competence. It can only measure consensus factors that tend to indicate competence, such as whether a candidate for certification is more or less likely to be competent. Further, attaining certification often reflects an individual's determination and diligence in seeking such status, undertaking the proper preparation, spending the time and money to apply, and so forth. Conversely, it is undeniable that many professionals who are universally recognized as competent by peers, clients, customers, or institutions have simply not sought certification in voluntary programs offered by nongovernmental organizations such as membership societies or boards affiliated with them. For a program to represent without qualification that "certified individuals are competent" may often imply that those not certified are not competent; that too can be misleading.

  ◆ It may not be possible in an examination setting to accurately and precisely measure competence. In fact, most individuals under-perform on certification examinations because an examination is usually taken in such an artificial environment. In the "real life" of professional practice, individuals have time to think, ask colleagues or supervisors for advice, conduct research, tentatively try reversible approaches and correct them if they don't work, and so on. The added pressures of anxiety, time, and other stresses that do not correlate directly with everyday professional endeavors are also present. Even a passing score allows some level of incorrect answers, so the entire process is not susceptible to an unqualified characterization as an accurate measure of competence. The reasons a person failed an examination may be related to proficiency in reading or other language skills, rather than skill in the subject area. These factors are likely more relevant in areas of professional practice where manual skill is primary.

◆ Little definitive guidance on whether certification equates with competence is available. In 1990, the U.S. Supreme Court *(Peel v. Attorney Registration and Disciplinary Comm'n.)* did address the meaning of certification in an analogous context, where the issue was the permissibility of advertising a lawyer's specialty area of practice. The court said: "A claim of certification is not an un-verifiable opinion of the ultimate quality of a lawyer's work or a promise of success, but is simply a fact, albeit one with multiple predicates, from which a consumer may or may not draw an inference of the likely qualities of an attorney's work in a given area of practice." A footnote to the Supreme Court's decision went on to say that "of course, many lawyers who do not have certification or do not publicize certification may, in fact, be more able than others who do claim such a credential." Thus, it is recognized that certification is only one factor in measuring competence, and it is by no means the determining factor.

◆ An examination by itself, or even a list of qualifications and criteria, cannot accurately measure competence. If psychometrically sound, examinations can be merely predictive of a tendency within a range to show that a person has demonstrated the knowledge or skill considered by consensus as necessary to perform certain professional functions.

• Certification provides only a tendency toward, not a guarantee of, competence; but that is valuable in and of itself. It could legitimately lead some to deal exclusively with certified professionals for employment, reimbursement, and other activities if only for reasons of convenience. But of course it should not lead anyone to conclude that only certified professionals are competent or that noncertified professionals are incompetent. For certification organizations, the focus on competence adds perceived value to their credentialing programs—but clearly does not give *carte blanche* to tout in promotional literature or other publications certification as a definitive measure of competence.

• Another distinction worth keeping in mind is that between a certification program and a "certificate program." Many organizations offer educational programming, whether day-long, weekend-long, or much longer in duration, which may or may not include testing at the end of the program but for which the attendees receive a written certificate indicating participation (or, where there is testing, the written certificate indicates that the individual has passed the test). This is to be distinguished from certification, which has come to be recognized as a more comprehensive measurement of an individual against criteria, standards or principles established by the profession and usually including elements of education, experience and testing. Those who complete a certificate program may legitimately and appropriately display their certificates and may refer to them on résumés or *curriculum vitae;* but they should be careful to avoid suggesting that they have completed professional certification.

Chapter 68 Resources

Books

Dorn. "Selected Areas of Law Affecting Private Credentialing Organizations." In *1999 Legal Symposium*. Washington, D.C.: American Society of Association Executives, 1999.

Glassie. "Key Precedents and Recent Developments in the Law of Credentialing." In *2002 DC Legal Symposium*. Washington, D.C.: American Society of Association Executives, 2002, p. 239.

Glassie and Hamm. "Certification and Accreditation Programs: Understanding the Risks." In *2002 DC Legal Symposium*. Washington, D.C.: American Society of Association Executives, 2002, p. 221.

Jacobs. "Antitrust and Other Legal Issues for Nonprofit Trade Associations." In *Nonprofit Governance and Management*. Chicago: American Bar Association and American Society of Corporate Secretaries, 2002, p. 563.

Jacobs and Glassie. *Certification and Accreditation Law Handbook, 2d ed.* Washington, D.C.: American Society of Association Executives, 2004.

Jacobs and Ogden. *Legal Risk Management for Associations.* Washington, D.C.: American Psychological Association, 1995, p. 63.

O'Neill. "An Overview of the Law of Private Credentialing." In *1999 Legal Symposium*. Washington, D.C.: American Society of Association Executives, 1999.

Schoon and Smith. *The Licensure and Certification Mission.* New York: Forbes, 2000.

Articles

Tenenbaum. "Risky Business? Certification and Accreditation Programs." *Association Law & Policy* (February 1, 2003).

Cases

Goldfarb v. Virginia State Bar, 421 U.S. 773 (1975). Illegality of attorney's minimum fee schedules.

National Soc'y of Professional Eng'rs v. United States, 435 U.S. 679 (1978). Illegality of ban on competitive bidding.

Salter v. New York State Psychological Ass'n, 198 N.E.2d 250 (N.Y. 1964). Denial of membership in society.

Falcone v. Middlesex County Medical Soc'y, 170 A.2d 791 (N.J. 1961). Denial of membership in society.

DeGregorio v. American Bd. of Internal Medicine, 844 F. Supp. 186 (D.N.J. 1994). Affirming legality of imposition of time-limited certification with required recertification.

Peel v. Attorney Registration and Disciplinary Comm'n., 496 U.S. 91 (1980).

Other Resources

FTC Advisory Opinion 350, 76 F.T.C. 1093 (1969). Accreditation program for producers.

FTC Advisory Opinion, 89 F.T.C. 654 (1977). Certification program for petroleum industry members.

FTC Advisory Opinion, 89 F.T.C. 668 (1977). Certification program for moving consultants.

FTC Advisory Opinion, 91 F.T.C. 1204 (1978). Certification program for pedorthics professionals.

FTC Advisory Opinion (Jan. 19, 1995). Accrediting standards for trade and technical schools.

DOJ Business Review Letter 78-21. Certification program for audio-visual specialists.

DOJ Business Review Letter 84-19. Accreditation of travel agents and clearinghouse for ticket sales.

DOJ Business Review Letter 86-2. Accreditation of travel schools.

DOJ Release of Oct. 31, 1978. Audio-visual specialist certification program.

Chapter 68A
Certification of Professionals— Administration

Professional certification programs assess whether individuals meet specified levels of education, experience, and knowledge in a profession or field according to consensus criteria, standards or principles of competence. Those who have the requisite credentials of eligibility and demonstrate that they have acquired the applicable professional "body of knowledge" are granted a credential, typically the right to state that they are certified in the area through use of a designation (legally, a certification mark; e.g., "Certified Association Executive" or its acronym "CAE"). Often a certificate is also granted, but certification does not constitute an academic degree, and thus the designation is not a title (e.g., Ph.D.).

The criteria, standards, or principles for certification typically include academic qualifications, experience in the profession or field, and passage of a written examination. Many certification programs also impose the requirement that those who have been certified must comply with a code of professional conduct. The written examination, though, is often the focus of the certification process since most applicants will not consider attempting to attain certification unless they have the requisite academic educational and professional experience backgrounds.

In order to develop and administer a psychometrically valid and legally defensible examination, a significant effort is required, usually involving preparation of a job analysis and/or role delineation study, careful development of an examination through question and answer item-writing workshops, and secure and objective administration of the exam in order to ensure accurate scores and protection of the integrity of the process.

Most often, consultants are engaged to provide professional assistance in the examination development and administration process, ranging from individual psychometricians to large companies with substantial experience in test development and administration.

Professional certification by a nonprofit nongovernmental body is perhaps the best method of self-regulation to avoid excessive government regulation. To the extent that certification programs use reasonable criteria, standards, or principles and are conducted with fairness and impartiality, they are likely to withstand government scrutiny and regulation. Therefore, associations involved in certification programs should take care to ensure they are aware of (or even ahead of) the rapid legal developments that could affect these activities.

The expenses for the development of a professional certification program, including consultant fees and costs, can be significant, but the revenues also can be substantial once certification becomes important for practice in a profession or field. The effort certainly requires dedication by association volunteers and staff. Although many other practical issues arise, a few of the more significant procedural or administrative issues are outlined in this chapter.

Summary

- Certification programs can give rise to legal claims from third parties on a number of bases, including due process, antitrust, discrimination, and tort liability. Common law fairness principles mandate that a certification program be substantively and procedurally fair and reasonable. Procedural due process is thus important in promoting substantive fairness, but is extremely relevant in making certain that any complaints or disciplinary matters are handled appropriately, and any appeals from such actions are legally defensible.

  - Legal actions can be brought by disgruntled or failed candidates, or those who are complained about and become the subject of disciplinary action for violation of the code of ethics, for example.

  - Such aggrieved individuals may sue on due process grounds, or may base their claims on antitrust violations, breach of contract, defamation, or tortious interference with business relations. Antitrust claims are legion, but in the context of a well-developed and administered certification program that is essentially pro-competitive, often are not successful.

- Another area of potential legal exposure is tort, that is, claims that the certification organization was negligent in some way that resulted in harm to a third party, such as a patient or customer of the certified professional. Although there are risks involved in all of these areas, careful planning and management of the program, together with appropriate insurance coverage, greatly minimizes the potential risk of liability.

- The fundamental bases of any nonprofit nongovernmental certification program are criteria, standards, or principles that are established as requirements for certification. Any challenge to the requirements will center on their validity. Do the criteria, standards, or principles required to attain the credential fairly represent the attributes necessary to practice competently in the profession or field? In mounting a legal defense for a certification program that is being challenged, one will typically attempt to demonstrate the essential validity of the program by explaining the careful process used to ensure that the program's requirements reflect, to the extent possible, consensus in the profession or field. Likewise, experts such as psychometricians will be utilized to explain why, in their judgment, the requirements together suggest a valid measurement of the level of competence for which the program is aimed.

- The best way to maximize validity is to have an open process by which all affected constituencies may participate and/or comment on the certification program as it is developed or when it is changed. A broad base of participation and input will help ensure that the requirements do not unfairly bias or discriminate against any eligible professionals and accurately measure competency. In determining if the criteria are reasonable, the following guidelines should be considered:

  - The criteria, standards, or principles should be no more stringent than necessary to ensure the levels of competency or quality that the program aims to measure have been achieved by the candidates (i.e., entry level, proficiency level, advanced level, etc.). This is particularly true when certification is of significant economic value, for example, as a prerequisite for employment or third-party reimbursement.

  - Any combination of reasonable education, experience, or examination requirements can be used as the bases for certification. However, it may be advisable to establish alternative criteria where requirements for certification are difficult or expensive for many potential candidates.

  - Criteria, standards, or principles for certification may include, and perhaps should include, continuing requirements and periodic reassessment of those previously certified.

- Criteria, standards, or principles should be established only after reasonable notice to all those who may be affected by certification requirements, including representatives of potential candidates and users of their services. Notice should include an opportunity to participate in establishing certification requirements, such as by commenting on proposed requirements.

- In addition to reasonable criteria, standards, or principles, any individual certification program should include policies and procedures ensuring that the criteria, standards, or principles are applied fairly to all candidates for certification. The following guidelines should be considered:

- Participation in a certification program ordinarily must be voluntary (except when government agencies authorize associations to administer programs that the agencies use for administering licensing, professional designation, or other mandatory government credentialing programs).

- ◆ Participation in a program should not be denied because a candidate is not a member of the certifying organization. However, fees charged to nonmembers for certification may be higher than those charged to members to reflect any members' dues or assessments that contribute to funding the program. There are no rigid guidelines, and virtually no precedent-setting court or agency pronouncements, on what is a fair and defensible nonmember fee increment. Certainly, where a professional certification program is subsidized by a related professional society, those who are not members of the society can be expected to pay some supplement for certification services to reflect the fact that they are no paying dues to the society. But beyond that questions remain, such as whether it is appropriate to reflect in the nonmember certification fees some amount to reflect the estimated value of society members' volunteer time dedicated to the certification program.

- ◆ It is not clear whether it is legal to summarily "grandfather" current organization members to a new certification program—that is, provide automatic certification without determining if the current members meet reasonable requirements—the legality will depend on the facts and circumstances in each case. The organizations that approve nongovernmental professional certifying bodies, the National Commission on Certifying Agencies (NCCA) of the National Organization for Competency Assurance and the American National Standards Institute (ANSI) disfavor grandfathering (see *Resources*).

- Organizations may promote their certification programs to potential participants or to the public as good measures for determining the qualifications of practicing individuals. However, they should not promote certified individuals by name (beyond directories and listings) or disparage the noncertified.

- Denial of certification should not be used to "blackball" individuals, to limit the number of competitors, or to otherwise arbitrarily deny potential applicants access to certification.

  - ◆ Denial of certification should be made by written notice to the applicant giving the reasons for denial; the candidate should be provided with an opportunity to respond, possibly at a hearing held for that purpose; in some circumstances it may be prudent to offer an appeal to the candidate, with the ultimate decision made by a body other than the one that made the original certification denial.

♦ Assessment of the qualifications of applicants for certification may be best made by an objective body or organization not composed exclusively of those who have received certification.

♦ All qualifying candidates should receive the same certification title or denomination for which they qualify, with no discrimination between organization members and nonmembers or any other arbitrary differentiation.

• A number of issues related to intellectual property arise in connection with a professional certification program. Specifically, there are legal issues with respect to copyright protection for examinations and related certification materials (such as exam items, candidate guides, brochures, applications, etc.), potential trade secret legal protection for exams, and trademark protection for the name of the certification organization/program and the certification mark used by those who are certified.

♦ When unpaid volunteers assist in creating examination items without compensation, there is a likelihood that those items can be claimed to be owned by their "creators," the volunteers. So volunteer exam writers should either receive stipends for their efforts pursuant to written engagements (rendering these efforts "work for hire" and presumed to be owned by the paying organization) or the organization should require written blanket copyright assignments from the volunteer exam writers. Volunteers or consultants who participate in creating examinations should also be required to agree in writing to confidentiality and to avoiding exploitation of their unique knowledge of the exams through exam preparation services or publications offered to candidates.

♦ Special secure procedures exist at the U.S. Library of Congress Copyright Office for obtaining copyright registration of certification exams. Other materials, such as booklets and instructions for candidates, should also be registered in the regular Copyright Office process.

♦ It is advisable to register the name and certification marks related to the program with the U.S. Patent and Trademark Office if possible (although acronyms and certification marks are not as easily registered as trade or service marks). Recent PTO decisions make certification mark registration by private nongovernmental certification bodies more likely than previously *(In re National Council for Therapeutic Recreation Certification, Inc.* and *In re The Council on Certification of Nurse Anesthetists).*

♦ The U.S. Supreme Court has affirmed the right of certified individuals, as a matter of constitutionally protected commercial speech, to advertise their certification as specialists (*Peel v. Attorney Registration and Disciplinary Commission*).

• It is important that governance of a certification program be sufficiently autonomous from a related, supporting, or sponsoring professional membership organization to ensure that no improper pressure or bias influences the credentialing decisions. Conflicts can derive from the fact that the certification body has a duty in part as a quasi-public entity, whereas the professional organization has duties primarily to its members. NCCA and ANSI have mandated "administrative independence" for certification programs, although this standard may be relaxed somewhat in specific cases. The essence of resolution of the issue is for there to be no direct or indirect undue influence from the membership organization to the body making credentialing decisions.

♦ Such independence is most easily accomplished by separate incorporation of the certification body, but this also risks the certification program eventually becoming totally separate and removing a potentially valuable revenue source for the membership organization. At a minimum, all decisions related to eligibility, standards, examinations, scoring, and appeals should be made in an autonomous manner by the certification body (i.e., its board or commission), and procedures should be in place to ensure this independence of action.

♦ Policies should also be in place to govern conflicts of interest, confidentiality, copyright, and so on.

• There are limitations on activities organizations can conduct based on their specific tax-exempt status under Section 501(c)(3) or Section 501(c)(6) of the Internal Revenue Code, respectively. Section 501(c)(3) organizations must be organized and operated primarily for charitable, educational, religious, or scientific purposes. Section 501(c)(6) organizations must be organized and operated to advance a type of business or profession as a whole. It is important to determine whether development and implementation of certification programs are consistent with Section 501(c)(3) purposes or Section 501(c)(6) purposes.

♦ Under the Internal Revenue Code and IRS regulations, educational purposes relate either to "the instruction or training of the individual for the purpose of improving or developing his capabilities; or . . . the instruction of the public on subjects useful to the individual and beneficial to the community." Examples of educational organizations include schools with regularly scheduled curriculums, museums, and organizations that present public discussion groups, forums, panels, lectures, or similar programs. In a series of revenue rulings, the IRS has provided further guidance on what types of activities are considered "educational" for these purposes.

◆ Pure instructional programs that provide training directly to individuals are of course considered educational in nature, as are organizations that publish and disseminate informational material that confers a benefit on the public as a whole. In addition, the IRS has found that an engineering society qualified for exemption under Section 501(c)(3) because its research was conducted for the benefit of, and distributed freely to, the general public.

◆ However, activities that primarily benefit the members of a given profession rather than the community at large will generally not be considered educational within the meaning of Section 501(c)(3). For example, in one ruling an association of investment clubs were found to not furthering educational and charitable purposes because "many of the activities [of the organization were] directed in whole or in part to the support and promotion of the economic interest of the investment clubs that comprise its membership." Also a nonprofit organization that administered peer review boards was not operated exclusively for charitable and educational purposes, because "its primary objective is to maintain the professional standards, prestige, and independence of the organized medical profession and thereby furthers the common business interest of the organization's members." Likewise, in a medical specialty board that devised and administered examinations to physicians did not qualify as a Section 501(c)(3) exempt organization because the organization's activities were considered to be directed primarily to serving interests of individual professionals.

◆ A city bar association conducted many bona fide educational activities, such as sponsoring educational seminars, publishing articles, maintaining speaker panels, and providing legal assistance to indigent individuals. However, the association also conducted activities that were "directed at the promotion and protection of the practice of law" and furthered the common business purposes of the members. IRS concluded that the existence of these non-educational purposes precluded designation of the association as a Section 501(c)(3) organization. Similarly, the IRS has held that a medical society that engaged in a variety of educational activities, but also provided a patient referral service and conducted public relations activities for the profession, was not operated exclusively for educational and charitable purposes.

- ◆ IRS officials have often interpreted standard setting and certification activities (even when conducted in conjunction with legitimate educational and training activities) as primarily advancing the business interests of a particular industry or of the individuals credentialed more consistent with a Section 501(c)(6) organization rather than one dedicated to the public interest under Section 501(c)(3). For example, in one ruling, product testing and certification activities were considered self-regulatory measure to prevent trade abuses in an industry and consistent with Section 501(c)(6) status. In another, testing, inspection, and certification program for products were considered activities in furtherance of improvement of business conditions and consistent with Section 501(c)(6) status. Elsewhere the IRS has challenged certification programs as inconsistent with Section 501(c)(3) status whether or not the certification activities are substantial in relation to the organization's budget. Thus, any significant formal testing and certification program could provide grounds for the IRS to revoke or deny Section 501(c)(3) status.

- • A 2004 private letter ruling by the IRS signaled a change in its position. Here a large Section 501(c)(3) organization conducted numerous activities, including operation of a professional certification program. Consistent with prior holdings, the IRS found that the certification activities were not "substantially related" to exempt purposes under Section 501(c)(3). The IRS took the position that an activity might be consistent with, appropriate for, and related to, Section 501(c)(6) activities, but nonetheless would not be "substantially related" to Section 501(c)(3) exempt purposes.

  - ◆ The IRS also found, however, that the certification program was "insubstantial" in comparison with the extensive activities of the organization and would not jeopardize its Section 501(c)(3) status. This appears to be a significant departure from previous IRS positions, in which any sort of a substantial or significant certification program would be held inconsistent with 501(c)(3) status and, thus, not appropriate to be conducted by such an organization. As a result, many Section 501(c)(3) organizations have now "spun off" their certification programs into Section 501(c)(6) entities as a reasonable way to protect the tax exempt status of the main organization.

  - ◆ Notably, though, because the program addressed in this ruling was also considered a "regularly carried on" trade or business, the IRS held that revenues from the certification program would be considered unrelated business income subject to tax ("UBIT") to the Section 501(c)(3) organization involved in the ruling. It is likely that many Section 501(c)(3) organizations have not been treating revenues from such exclusively (c)(6) activities as UBIT, but rather considering them simply insubstantial although not taxable. In addition, the ruling is noteworthy because it concludes that an insubstantial professional certification program will not jeopardize the main organization's Section 501(c)(3) status. The ruling does not discuss what specific factors led the IRS to conclude the program was insubstantial, that is, whether revenues, budget amounts, size of staff, and so on, were determinative. The IRS does not, however, direct that such a program be carved out and separated from the Section 501(c)(3) organization.

◆ This position has important implications for any Section 501(c)(3) organization conducting activities that might be characterized as predominantly in furtherance of (c)(6), but not (c)(3), purposes, including, but not limited to, professional certification. It should be emphasized, too, that a private letter ruling such as this one is explicitly not considered to be precedent binding upon the IRS nor the basis for reliance by other exempt organizations beyond the one for which the ruling was issued.

• Another important yet unique aspect of the legal analysis involves certification programs that have been developed pursuant to a direct or indirect governmental mandate. Where the certification activity arguably "lessens the burdens of government," the IRS has at times granted Section 501(c)(3) status. An important case is in this regard is one in which an Indiana university, which previously had performed agricultural regulatory functions on behalf of the state, delegated to a private nonprofit association the responsibility of seed certification in accordance with Indiana and federal law. The association also conducted research and educational activities.

◆ The court found that the association's certification activities were in furtherance of an exempt charitable purpose under Section 501(c)(3) because the association lessened the burden of government. There is also and IRS ruling in which preparation of test format to be used by state registration boards was found to not involve the instruction or training of individuals and therefore not "educational" within the meaning of Section 501(c)(3), but constituting "lessening the burdens of government" provided that the organization's governing documents reflected such purposes and the organization was not formed to support another non-Section 501(c)(3) organization.

◆ Where a certification program is developed and conducted pursuant to requirements in federal or state law, it will be reasonable to take the position that the program lessens the burdens of government and should be consistent with Section 501(c)(3). It should be noted, however, that lessening the burdens of government as a ground for supporting Section 501(c)(3) status has not, as a general matter, been recently favored by the IRS.

Chapter 68A Resources

Books

Cipriani. "Contracting for Certification Services." In *Associations and the Law*. Jacobs, ed. Washington, D.C.: American Society of Association Executives, 2002, p. 86.

Fellman. "How to Implement and Enforce an Effective Professional Certification Program." In *2000 Legal Symposium*. Washington, D.C.: American Society of Association Executives, 2000.

Jacobs and Glassie. *Certification and Accreditation Law Handbook, 2d ed.* Washington, D.C.: American Society of Association Executives, 2004.

Jacobs and Ogden. *Legal Risk Management for Associations.* Washington, D.C.: American Psychological Association, 1995, p. 63.

Peluso. "The Certification Examination Process." In *1999 Legal Symposium*. Washington, D.C.: American Society of Association Executives, 1999.

Articles

Cobb and Tai. "IRS Determines Certification Programs Constitute Unrelated Trade or Business for Section 501(c)(3) Organizations." *Association Law & Policy* (July, 2005).

Cases

DeGregorio v. American Bd. of Internal Medicine, 844 F. Supp. 186 (D.N.J. 1994). Affirming legality of imposition of time-limited certification with required recertification.

Peel v. Attorney Registration and Disciplinary Comm'n, 496 U.S. 91 (1980).

Jamie Ambrose v. New England Ass'n. of Schools and Colleges, Inc., 252 F.3d 488 (1st Cir. 2001). Unsuccessful suit by students for improperly accrediting their college.

Hand v. American Board for Surgery, Inc., 2002 U.S. Dist. LEXIS 2323, 2002 WL 227174 (E.D. Pa. 2002). Court upholds denial of certification, finding no unfairness in criteria or process.

Indiana Crop Improvement Assn. v. Commissioner of Internal Revenue, 76 T.C. 394 (1981). Finding of Section 501(c)(3) status for an agricultural certification organization authorized by the state government to conduct certification.

In re National Council for Therapeutic Recreation Certification, Inc., Trademark Trial and Appeal Board, Serial No. 75701344. September 15, 2006. Granting of certification mark registration for professional certification program denomination.

In re The Council on Certification of Nurse Anesthetists, Trademark Trial and Appeal Board, Serial No. 75722091. March 22, 2007. Granting of certification mark registration for professional certification program denomination.

Other Resources

FTC Advisory Opinion 350, 76 F.T.C. 1093 (1969). Accreditation program for producers.

FTC Advisory Opinion, 89 F.T.C. 654 (1977). Certification program for petroleum industry members.

FTC Advisory Opinion, 89 F.T.C. 668 (1977). Certification program for moving consultants.

FTC Advisory Opinion, 91 F.T.C. 1204 (1978). Certification program for pedorthics professionals.

FTC Advisory Opinion (Jan. 19, 1995). Accrediting standards for trade and technical schools.

DOJ Business Review Letter 78–21. Certification program for audio-visual specialists.

DOJ Business Review Letter 84–19. Accreditation of travel agents and clearinghouse for ticket sales.

DOJ Business Review Letter 86-2. Accreditation of travel schools.

DOJ Release of Oct. 31, 1978. Audio-visual specialist certification program.

Treas. Reg. 1.501(c)(3)-1(d)(3). Pronouncement re public education.

Revenue Ruling 77-272, 1977-CB 191. Ruling held that organization providing apprenticeship training programs to Native Americans furthers educational purposes.

Revenue Ruling 71–506, 1971–2 CB 233. Ruling on exemption of an engineering society where its publications were available to the public.

Revenue Ruling 76–386, 1976–2 CB 144. Ruling in which investment club association was denied exemption.

Revenue Ruling 74–553, 1974–2 CB 168. Ruling on organization of peer review programs.

Revenue Ruling 73-567, 1973–2 CB 178. Medical specialty board exemption.

Revenue Ruling 71-505, 1971–2 CB 232. City bar association denied Section 501(c)(3) exemption because of services promoting members.

Revenue Ruling 71–504, 1971–2 CB 231. Patient referral and other activities precluded a medical society from attaining Section 501(c)(3) exemption.

Revenue Ruling 70–187, 1970–X CB 131. Product testing and certification not consistent with Section 501(c)(3).

G.C.M. 38459, July 31, 1980. Publication of weekly periodical and scholarly articles furthers educational purposes.

G.C.M. 8315046, January 12, 1983. Testing, inspection and certification program not consistent with Section 501(c)(3) exemption.

G.C.M. 37222, August 19, 1977. Preparation of test formats lessens the burdens of government and therefore qualifies as Section 501(c)(3) activity.

P.L.R. 200439043. The professional certification program of a large Section 501(c))(3) organization was found to be subject to unrelated business income but, in this case, so insubstantial as to not defeat exemption in this classification.

National Organization for Competency Assurance. "ANSI-NOCA 1100—Standard Assessment-Based Certification Programs: An American National Standard," March, 2009.

National Commission for Certifying Agencies, "Standards for the Accreditation of Certification Programs." December, 2007.

Chapter 81A
Joint Ventures with Businesses

Beyond subsidiaries, in which the tax-exempt main organization essentially owns and controls another entity, many associations and other nonprofit organizations have found that joint venturing, affiliating or "partnering" with business organizations—those which they do not own or control—can have advantages in developing or operating programs that are of benefit to members or other constituents. One common approach is for the exempt organization to merely sponsor or endorse the products or services of a business to the exempt organization's constituency; those sponsorship programs are very common for insurance, credit cards, and other products or services. Their unique tax ramifications are considered in another chapter. But sometimes it is seen as more desirable, and more lucrative to the exempt organization, to "share" the development, management, promotion, and financing of a program or activity with a business corporation. Allied taxable business corporations may bring capitalization, entrepreneurship, marketing, or other resources to a joint endeavor serving the association's constituencies. And the joint development and operation of a project, program, service, event, or endeavor can help spread the risk between the association and its affiliate or "partner." Most important, through a joint venture—type arrangement, the exempt organization can maintain partial ownership in a program or activity developed and operated jointly with a commercial business, not just passively sponsor or endorse the program or activity. There tends to be more "buy-in" and enthusiasm when the exempt organization actually participates in owning and running the endeavor, both at the organization and among its constituents. Ultimately, the organization's ownership interest in the venture can became a considerable asset that might generate income over the long term or some day be sold.

This chapter considers structure and tax-exemption aspects of joint ventures with businesses.

Summary

- Beyond consideration of owned and controlled subsidiaries of associations and other exempt organization "parents," there are many instances in which the exempt organization will want to "partner" with an existing taxable business entity. Sponsorship or endorsement of a commercial business is a conventional approach to working with a business; it can reap significant rewards for the association or other exempt organization (and is addressed in another chapter). But often the exempt organization will want to share ownership, including profits and losses, with the business. This is especially common when some new program or activity is created together by the exempt organization and the business. An example might include a situation in which a membership association and a software company get together in a plan in which the company develops custom software for the field represented by the association with the two entities jointly owning the software and with the association marketing and promoting the software to its membership. Another example might be a trade show or exhibition owned jointly by an exempt organization and a commercial exhibition management company. These arrangements are often called "joint ventures."

• While the terms "partner," "partnering," and "partnership" are used often in this context, it is highly desirable from a legal point of view to avoid using those terms in actual documentation of the relationship of an exempt organization with a taxable business. That is because the law implies a myriad of often vague and archaic ramifications to the structure of a legal "partnership" which, without careful examination and consideration, might not be the intent of either the exempt organization or the business in forming and operating their endeavor together. Better to call the relationship a "joint venture," an "affiliation," or something similar.

• A joint venture is the typical vehicle to use when an exempt organization and business corporation (or even in some cases another exempt organization) decide to "share" some program or activity. Typical specific legal structures available for these arrangements include:

   ◆ Contract joint venture. This is an agreement between the sharing entities on ownership, purposes, control, costs, profits, losses, termination, and other aspects of a shared endeavor. It provides no special limitation or additional protection for the joint venture participants from liability arising from the endeavor. But it is a simple, efficient, low-maintenance, non-statutory approach that is therefore very flexible. Whatever the parties decide with respect to the various aspects of "sharing" in the program or activity is likely to be legally binding and enforceable.

   ◆ Limited liability company ("LLC"). This is a separate state-chartered entity, technically a membership company, not an equity corporation, which has many attributes of a business corporation. Most important, an LLC provides a strong liability "shield" for its owners (called "members") equivalent to the protection afforded shareholders of corporations (who, like LLC members, usually cannot be claimed liable individually for the debts and obligations of the entity). This distinguishes an LLC dramatically from a contract joint venture, where there is no such liability "shield." An

LLC can avoid taxation at the entity level and be structured so that only the members are subject to taxation on the net revenues of the LLC. That means that the tax-exempt organization member of an LLC could avoid taxation completely on its share of the revenues in many circumstances (in particular, where the activities of the LLC which generate net revenues are consistent with the exempt status of the organization, e.g., a jointly owned and operated journal or exhibition). An LLC can have a bylaws—type governing document, often called the "Operating Agreement," that establishes its ownership shares, governance, termination provisions, and so on. An LLC can have a Board of Directors-type governing body, often called a "Board of Managers." All in all, an LLC is likely the most-utilized legal structure for affiliations, "partnerships," or other kinds of joint venture relationships between exempt organizations and business corporations.

◆ Tax-exempt nonprofit corporation. This is the same kind of entity used by most trade associations, professional societies, cause organizations, charities, and other nonprofit organizations. It is a separate state-chartered entity that is ordinarily prohibited from issuing equity stock; there is, therefore, no true "ownership" of the entity. It does provide liability protection for the members (just as any other nonprofit organization). If it is organized and operated consistent with the IRS requirements for tax-exempt organizations, it too can qualify for exemption. The major drawback is that this kind of organization is not "owned and controlled" in any regular respect; it is therefore not usually suitable for an affiliation, "partnership," or joint venture between a tax-exempt organization and a business corporation.

◆ Taxable business corporation. This is a conventional equity corporation (often called a "C corporation") ultimately equivalent to that of General Motors or other businesses large and small. It has the major advantage of providing a liability shield for the "owners" or shareholders. And it provides an easy mechanism for ownership and control; the entities that are "sharing" some program or activity each become shareholders of the corporation. The major disadvantage to this kind of entity in the association/business joint venture context is that it is separately taxed as an entity; there is therefore a kind of "double taxation" in which the entity is first taxed and then an owner/shareholder, which is a taxable entity, is taxed on its dividends. A C corporation is thus usually less attractive than an LLC.

• Ultimately a contract joint venture agreement or limited liability company present the most attractive two alternatives in "partnering" with a business corporation to own and operate a program or activity together. The difference is principally in whether the liability shield of the LLC is worth the extra effort in forming a new entity. In either a joint venture agreement or LLC Operating Agreement, a few terms should be addressed to the mutual satisfaction of both the exempt organization and business corporation:

- The name of the endeavor

- The ownership interests of the parties

- Composition, recruitment, leadership, and role of whatever committee or board will be in charge

- Capitalization requirements for each party

- Possible recapitalization or "cash calls"

- Ownership rights, both during and after the endeavor, in intellectual property created by the endeavor

- Licensing by the endeavor of non-exclusive rights to each party's name, logo, or other intellectual property

- Confidentiality

- Whether and how other parties might be permitted to participate

- The tax treatment of the endeavor

- The detailed singular obligations of each party, possibly with "service standard" provisions

- Audit and accounting provisions

- Termination for breach following notice and opportunity to "cure" for the allegedly breaching party

- Termination without breach, possibly including some "buy-sell" or "auction sale" provisions

- Resolution of disputes

- Means for amending the arrangements

- A very important consideration in any association/business "sharing" of a program or activity is the effect on the federal income tax exemption status of the participating association or other exempt organization. If the joint venture's programs or activities are such that the net income would be subject to UBIT if conducted by the participating exempt organization, of course, they will also likely be subject to UBIT taxation as well for the exempt organization if conducted through a contract joint venture or LLC (and would certainly be subject to taxation at the entity level, no matter what are the activities, if conducted through a C corporation). But if the joint venture's programs or activities would be eligible for tax exempt treatment if conducted solely by the exempt organization and within its structure, the question arises whether that exempt treatment is lost by virtue of sharing in the programs or activities with a taxable business corporation "partner" in the endeavors.

◆ For many years the answer was "yes" in many instances. The IRS long took the position that revenue to an exempt organization received through a joint venture between the exempt organization and a taxable business corporation, even if subject to exempt treatment if conducted by the exempt organization directly, lost the benefit of that treatment in a joint venture unless the exempt organization controlled the venture. Whether there was sufficient control to avoid taxation of the revenue to the exempt organization depended upon a variety of factors, no one of which was determinative—majority ownership by the exempt organization, majority seats on the governing board for the exempt organization, and so on (see Sanders article in Resources).

◆ In 2004, the IRS issued a ruling that provides more flexibility in these situations. The Service opined on a situation in which a tax-exempt university partnered with a commercial distance learning company to provide online education. Here the university did not own more than half of the venture nor control the governing board. But the university did instead have complete discretion, through exclusive veto power, over the curriculum and faculty of the venture. The IRS concluded that the university had authority over those aspects of the arrangement that related most closely to the university's tax-exempt purposes, education. And it permitted the university to receive net revenue from the "shared" venture on a tax-exempt basis. Although as always this ruling has no specific "precedent" value—it cannot be relied upon by other exempt organizations—it provides a useful view of the attitude and approach that the IRS can be expected to take in the situation of an exempt organization that shares a program or activity with a business corporation. Only if the exempt organization controls the whole venture (as was long the IRS position), or if it controls at least those aspects of the venture that relate to organization's exempt purposes, will the organization's share of the revenue likely enjoy exemption from federal income tax.

• One additional consideration is that of public disclosure. The Form 990 annual informational return revised in 2007–8 requires disclosure of joint venture–type arrangements in many circumstances.

Moreover, in its governance provisions, Form 990 (2008) asks whether the filing organization has any joint ventures or other similar arrangements with taxable businesses and, if so, whether the organization has a policy in place to evaluate the ramifications for the organization's federal income tax-exempt status. Since these tax returns are public documents, available from the IRS, on public interest Web sites, or from the filing organizations themselves, one can expect the information on these returns to be readily available to the organizations' constituencies, the press, to competitors, and to others.

• Joint ventures entered into with businesses have many advantages for exempt organizations. If properly formed and run, they provide a vehicle for sharing capitalization, ownership, marketing, and management of a program or activity with a commercial firm while still preserving tax exemption for the organization's share of net revenue. They deserve thorough exploration and consideration when an organization is planning a new or upgraded service for its constituency. But they are also complex undertakings which must be developed carefully with expert legal and tax assistance.

Chapter 81A Resources

Books

ABA Committee on Nonprofit Corporations. *Guide for Directors of Nonprofit Corporations, 2d ed*. Chicago: American Bar Association Section of Business Law, 2002, p. 91.

Cipriani. "Establishing an Affiliated Organization." In *Associations and the Law*. Jacobs, ed. Washington, D.C.: American Society of Association Executives, 2002, p. 114.

Hopkins. *The Law of Tax-Exempt Organizations, 8th ed*. Hoboken, N.J.: John Wiley, 2003, p. 918; 2006 Cum. Supp. 157.

Sanders. "Tax Planning for Joint Ventures: How to Use For-Profit Subsidiaries." In *1999 Legal Symposium*. Washington, D.C.: American Society of Association Executives, 1999.

Other

Internal Revenue Service Form 990 (2008), Part VI. Requirement for disclosure of whether there are joint ventures or other similar arrangements and, if so, whether there is a policy to evaluate the tax exemption ramifications.

Revenue Ruling 2004-51. IRS ruling that an exempt organization in a joint venture with a business corporation must at least control those elements of the venture which related to the exempt purposes of the organization.

Chapter 86A
Group Tax Exemption

Chapters, affiliates, and similar regional, state, and local organizations related to a central association or other nonprofit tax-exempt organizations may together obtain determinations that all related affiliated organizations are exempt from federal income tax. The group tax exemption process at the Internal Revenue Service ("IRS") is relatively simple, requiring the central organization to submit a group exemption application letter to the IRS. The central organization also must annually file a list of its qualifying tax-exempt affiliates or chapters. This listing is essentially an attestation by the central organization that its affiliates continue to qualify as tax-exempt organizations, which in turn relieves the IRS of its obligation to independently evaluate or reevaluate whether each chapter or affiliate qualifies for exemption. The principal advantage of group exemptions is that each chapter or affiliate covered by a group exemption letter, called a "subordinate" organization, is not obligated to go through the often burdensome and costly process of filing its own tax exemption application. There is also the opportunity, although not a requirement, that the related subordinate organizations may collectively file their annual informational tax returns with the IRS.

There are some disadvantages to group exemption, such as the inability of affiliates to individually obtain separate IRS determination letters regarding their tax exemption, the lack of separate assessments of the publicly supported status of subordinate charitable organizations, and the possibility that the central organization could be accused of being liable for the wrongful acts of one or more of its subordinate organizations. Despite these relatively minor drawbacks, group exemptions can be quite beneficial to both central organizations and to their chapters or affiliates; the streamlined process saves organizations significant amounts of money, effort, and time, allowing them to focus on their tax-exempt missions.

Summary

- The IRS recognizes a group of organizations as tax exempt if they are affiliated with a central organization. The affiliates, often called "chapters," usually have similar structures, goals, and activities.

- Group exemption serves as an administrative convenience for both the IRS and the affected organizations. Subordinate organizations are not required to file separate exemption applications, and thus the IRS is relieved of its obligation to process those applications.

- The central organization itself need not have received a determination by the IRS that it is tax exempt before it pursues a group exemption. Rather, a central organization may submit a group exemption request at the same time that it submits it own application for exemption.

- To apply for a group exemption, the central organization submits a group exemption application letter to the IRS on behalf of its chapters or affiliates. Assuming that the central organization has acquired recognition of its own tax-exempt status, this application must be signed by a principal officer of the central organization and must contain the central organization's employer identification number, the date of the letter recognizing its own tax-exempt status, and identification of the IRS office that issued that letter. In the group exemption application letter, the central organization must confirm the following information concerning all of its subordinate organizations intended to be covered by the group exemption:

  - They are affiliated with the central organization.

  - They are under its control or subject to its general supervision.

  - They all qualify for tax exemption under the same section of the Internal Revenue Code, but that section may be different from that of the central organization. For example, a central organization may be tax exempt as a charity, while all of its affiliates are exempt as social welfare organizations.

  - If they are not to be included in group returns, they are on the same accounting period as the central organization.

  - They are neither private foundations nor foreign corporations.

  - They were formed within the 15-month period before the date of submission of the group exemption application letter.

- The application letter must also contain, or include as attachments, the following:

  - A detailed description of the subordinate organizations' principal purposes and activities, including financial information;

  - A sample copy of a uniform governing instrument adopted by the subordinate organizations (such as model articles of incorporation or bylaws);

  - An affirmation that, to the best of the central organization officer's knowledge, the subordinate organizations are operating in accordance with the stated purposes;

- ◆ A statement that each subordinate organization to be included in the group exemption has provided written authorization to that effect to the central organization;

- ◆ A list of subordinate organizations to be included in the group exemption letter to which the IRS has previously issued a ruling or determination letter regarding tax exemption;

- ◆ If relevant, an affirmation that no subordinate organization to be covered by the group exemption is a private foundation; and

- ◆ A list of the names, addresses, and employer identification numbers of the subordinate organizations to be included in the group exemption letter.

- • Once these conditions are met, the IRS will determine whether the subordinate organizations qualify collectively for federal income tax exemption. If so, the IRS will issue a group exemption letter to the central organization.

- • It is permissible for a central organization to participate in more than one group exemption arrangement, such as having both charitable and social welfare affiliates.

- • A central organization may also be considered a subordinate organization with respect to a different central organization. For example, a state organization associated with a national organization may have subordinate local organizations covered by a group exemption.

- • In order to maintain a group exemption letter, the central organization is required to update the IRS annually on new subordinates to be included in the group exemption, subordinates no longer to be included in the group exemption, and subordinates that have changed their information. Specifically, the IRS must be apprised of:

  - ◆ Any changes in the purposes, character, or method of operation of the subordinate organizations to be included in the group exemption;

  - ◆ A separate list of the names, addresses, and employee identification numbers of the subordinate organizations for each of the following categories: (1) subordinates that have changed their names or addresses during the year, (2) subordinates that for any reason are no longer to be covered by the group exemption letter, and (3) subordinates that for any reason are to be added to the group exemption; and

  - ◆ With respect to new subordinate organizations to be added to the group, the information that must be submitted by a central organization initially on behalf of subordinates to be included in the group exemption.

- The group exemption process does not mandate that subordinate organizations and their central organization file the Form 990 (or 990-EZ) annual informational tax return together. In fact, the majority of national nonprofit organizations that use group exemptions require their affiliates to file their own annual returns.

- However, it is permissible for a central organization to file a group return on behalf of some or all of its subordinate organizations. If the central organization files only on behalf of some, rather than all of its subordinates, then it must attach a list of the subordinates included in the return.

- When a group exemption letter is terminated, then all of the subordinate organizations lose their tax-exempt status.

- A group exemption letter may be terminated in two basic ways:

  ◆ The central organization dissolves or otherwise ceases to exist.

  ◆ The central organization itself fails to continue to qualify as a tax-exempt organization, to submit the information necessary for group exemption, to file the annual information return, or to otherwise satisfy the reporting conditions.

- If continuing recognition of tax-exempt status is still desired despite termination of the group exemption, each subordinate organization must then file an application for determination of tax exemption, the central organization must file a new group exemption application letter, or the affiliates must become tax-exempt because of their relationship to a different qualifying central organization.

- The continued viability of a group exemption as applied to a specific subordinate organization is also dependent on the subordinate's continued compliance with the rules for group exemption inclusion, the authorization for inclusion, as well as the annual filing of any required information return for the subordinate.

- Loss of tax exemption by one or more affiliates of the group does not negatively impact the other members' group exemption status.

- The disadvantages to group exemptions include:

  ◆ Affiliates do not individually have separate IRS determination letters regarding their tax exemption, which can both complicate the process for obtaining tax exemptions on the state level and result in problems for Section 501(c)(3) charitable organizations. For example, donors often want the assurance that a determination letter provides, so as not to rely solely on the organization's representation that it is in fact a charitable entity.

♦ There is no separate assessment of the publicly supported status of subordinate charitable organizations, which may make it more difficult to assure donors or grant-making bodies that the prospective recipient of contributions or grants is a public or publicly supported charity.

♦ If a group member is found liable for legal liability or damages, there is a possibility that the group exemption will be used to support the argument that the central organization is liable as well, since in obtaining a group exemption the central organization must assert that it exercises some element of control over the subordinate organizations. This may not be a serious risk, but its assessment depends on an evaluation of all of the facts and circumstances in the accusation of liability of the central organization.

• Even though there are some disadvantages, if a main organization supervises or controls many chapters or affiliates that are very similar to each other, then use of the group exemption should be seriously considered. In addition to being efficient and convenient, the group exemption process is fairly straightforward and has virtually the same ramifications as an individual exemption.

Chapter 86A Resources

Books

Hopkins. *The Law of Tax Exempt Organizations.* New York: John Wiley, 2007, sec. 25.6.

Tenenbaum. *Association Tax Compliance Guide.* Washington, D.C.: American Society of Association Executives, 2000, pp. 13-16.

Other Resources

Revenue Procedure 80-27, 1980-1 CB 677.

Publication 4573 (Rev. 6-2007).

Planning Tax-Exempt Organizations. Matthew Bender & Company, ed., 2009, § 33.04.

Updated Chapters

Chapter 30
Contracts with Hotels & Convention Centers

Methods of making arrangements for meetings, seminars, and conventions at hotels, conference centers, convention centers, or other facilities vary widely from one nonprofit organization or association to another and from one meeting facility to another. Small meetings obviously require fewer arrangements than do large meetings. Meetings combined with trade shows, tours, or other activities are more complicated in their arrangements. This chapter concerns itself with only certain legal aspects of contracting for the use of meeting space.

Arrangements for meeting facilities always should be made or confirmed in writing, even for the smallest meetings. This should be done in such a way that a binding contract exists between the organization and the meeting facility management. Mere oral contracts for meeting facilities may not be enforceable. They should always be avoided.

Meeting cancellation insurance and insurance for liability arising from meetings should be considered.

Summary

- Contracts for the use of meeting facilities should be made sufficiently in advance of meeting dates to ensure the availability of adequate facilities and to allow time to communicate and confirm the terms in writing.

- Contract terms for meeting facilities ordinarily are discussed initially by telephone or in person. They should always be made the subject of a subsequent written contract between the organization and the facility management.

- Oral contracts for the use of meeting facilities can give rise to misunderstandings, may not always be legally enforceable, and should be avoided.

- A written contract for the use of meeting facilities can be made in a formal contract document or merely in an informal exchange of correspondence between an organization and a meeting facility. The latter approach is becoming less and less common as most managers of meeting facilities require formal written contracts.

- For an exchange of correspondence to become a binding, enforceable contract between an organization and a meeting facility, there must be at least a clear offer and acceptance of the specific terms of the arrangements. Typically, the arrangements are discussed and negotiated by phone or in person. The organization or the meeting facility then confirms the arrangements by letter. The recipient of the letter should acknowledge and assent to those stipulated arrangements. If the recipient makes changes, these changes should be agreed to in writing by whomever made the original proposal.

- Note that there are many subtleties and nuances to contract law. State statutes and decisions differ on fine points. By all means, organizations should consult with their legal counsel for assistance in effecting valid, binding contracts for meeting facilities.

- The organization should make certain that the representative of the meeting facility has authority to make a written agreement concerning the arrangements.

- Once a written agreement is made, it should not be changed except by further written agreement of both the organization and the meeting facility management.

- Most hotels and other managers of meeting facilities now require the use of a standard form contract to book meetings. These form contracts usually are drawn primarily for the protection of the meeting facility. They should be particularly well scrutinized by an organization and its legal counsel before the association signs. The organization should not feel apprehension or reluctance about attempting to negotiate changes in a standard form contract offered by a meeting facility.

- Some meeting facilities impose singularly onerous obligations on organizations when it becomes necessary to cancel or reschedule a meeting. These conditions should never be accepted unless the organization is certain it will be able to comfortably handle the terms for cancellation or rescheduling.

- When the commitment to use one meeting facility, such as a hotel, depends on the simultaneous availability of another facility, such as a convention center, care should be taken to ensure the arrangements with each facility are dependent on the arrangements with the other—if one facility becomes unavailable, the obligation to use the other should extinguish without obligation.

- Any meeting facility contract that imposes penalties for cancellation by the organization should impose at least as onerous penalties for cancellation by the facility.

- Care should be taken to distinguish between a hotel blocking in which the hotel agrees to set aside rooms in return for the organization's recommending those rooms to potential meeting attendees and a hotel blocking in which the organization commits to use and pay for the rooms. Any contract that confuses the two concepts should be clarified or rejected.

- Written agreements about arrangements for meeting facilities may contain specific terms for any aspects of the meetings or the facilities, including

  ◆ Meeting dates

  ◆ Anticipated participants and spouses

  ◆ Estimated numbers and types of rooms needed

  ◆ Prices of rooms

  ◆ Assurance of lowest room prices available to any guests at the time of the meeting

  ◆ Holding of rooms for late arrivals

  ◆ Cutoff date after which a specific number of rooms will be guaranteed

  ◆ Escape clause allowing the organization to cancel well before stipulated dates without any obligation

  ◆ Arrangements for organization approval of suite requests by meeting attendees

  ◆ Arrangements for early check-ins or stay-overs at reduced rates

  ◆ Promotion and publicity of meetings

  ◆ Firm or estimated prices for functions (with or without escalation clauses as meeting dates approach)

  ◆ Local taxes

  ◆ Gratuities

  ◆ Use of a master charge account

  ◆ Payment terms for the organization conducting the meeting

  ◆ Deposits by meeting participants

  ◆ Use of credit cards and check cashing by meeting participants

  ◆ Transportation to and from airports to meeting facilities

  ◆ Local transportation during the meetings

  ◆ Complimentary rooms and staff offices at meeting facility

- Conferences between the organization and facility staffs before the meetings

- Daily conferences with facility staffs during meetings

- Availability of additional meeting facility personnel at registration, checkout, restaurants, cocktail lounges, and other locations.

- Availability and full functioning of all regular food, entertainment, recreation, and transportation facilities for members

- Procedures and payments if members are "walked" (i.e., denied accommodations despite confirmed or guaranteed reservations)

- Numbers and types of meeting rooms

- Exhibit space

- Registration space

- Audiovisual equipment and facilities

- Meeting room sound, lighting, heating, and air conditioning, as well as availability of meeting facility staff to adjust these when necessary

- Use of outside services by the organization

- Entertainment

- Food and beverage service

- Labor costs

- Security service

- Fire drills for employees

- Fire protection equipment

- Frequency with which the facility is patrolled

- Kinds of locks on doors

- Cancellation because of strike, natural disaster, failure of mass transportation, and so forth

- Specific improvements at facility guaranteed before the meeting

- Assurance that no major construction will occur on the premises during the meeting except for unforeseen emergencies

- Assignability of the contract for meeting facilities if management or ownership of facilities changes before the meeting dates

◆ Maintenance of adequate liability insurance by the meeting facility

◆ Stipulated damages for failure of the meeting facility to provide agreed-upon rooms or other agreed-upon services

◆ Final occupancy report for the organization after the meeting

• There is typically a range of flexibility in negotiating hotel and convention center agreements that depends on a variety of factors, including the size of the event, the history of the organization's relationship with the property(ies) or chain(s), and the state of the hotel industry "market." Where an organization is able to negotiate terms more favorable than those on the prepared or standard hotel or convention center agreement form, the following are some possible areas of focus or goals in the negotiations. Note that it is unrealistic to expect to achieve all, or even most, of these; however, they do provide a list of goals to aspire to in each negotiation, especially for major events.

  ◆ *Attrition.* A hotel attrition provision should state that the hotel will allow a percentage attrition from the anticipated room block before the organization incurs any fees or damages. The percentage should be the highest that can be negotiated (often 10 percent up to 25 percent). Attrition penalties would therefore apply only if the organization fails to book its anticipated room block less the attrition "allowance."

  ◆ *Mitigation.* A mitigation provision should require a hotel to make all reasonable efforts to resell any unused rooms. The organization should not be responsible for attrition or cancellation penalties if the hotel meets or exceeds its average historic occupancy for the event period. Mitigation should not be based on the hotel achieving 100 percent occupancy.

  ◆ *Force majeure.* The organization should not be liable for attrition and cancellation penalties with a hotel or convention center if a force majeure situation occurs that the organization could not have reasonably foreseen. Force majeure provisions should include serious economic hardship for the organization, its constituency, or the general economy.

  ◆ *Audit.* Audit provisions should permit the organization to have access in confidence to the hotel's registrant list for the event period to confirm the hotel's mitigation efforts and to ensure that credit is received for the organization's meeting attendees who are staying at the hotel but booked outside the room block.

♦ *Hotel cancellation.* If the hotel cancels ("walks") any reservations in the organization's room block at a time when cancellation penalties for the organization would apply, the hotel should be required to pay these same penalties to the organization on a pro rata basis, in addition to total costs of rebooking, making alternative arrangements, and any related costs.

♦ *Construction.* A hotel or convention center should notify the organization in advance of non-emergency construction in public areas during the event period. If the organization determines that construction will cause a material interference with the event, the organization should be free to cancel without charge, with the hotel or convention center paying penalties for its de facto cancellation.

♦ *Rate guaranty.* Room rates applicable to the event should be subject to reduction to reflect any lower rates applicable during the event period that are advertised or granted by the hotel, with the hotel certifying the organization's "most favored customer" status prior to final payment from the organization.

♦ *Availability of convention center.* The organization should have the right to cancel each hotel booking at any time without penalty if the convention center co-booked for the event becomes unavailable for any reason.

♦ *Unauthorized agent.* The hotel should make best efforts to avoid booking for the event period through a booking or housing agent making unauthorized representations regarding authority from the organization or infringing on the organization's trademarks.

♦ *Change in management/ownership.* The hotel or convention center should be required to notify the organization of any major change in management or ownership, with the organization having the right to cancel without penalty if the change, in the organization's discretion, will materially affect the desirability or level of service of the facility.

• Insurance may be available to cover expenses and lost revenue resulting from cancellation of major meetings, including conventions, trade shows, and exhibits. A major meeting usually represents an enormous investment for an organization, especially if a trade show or exhibit is included. It also represents one of the major revenue sources for most organizations. Calamities such as a strike, fire, roof collapse, disease outbreak, or breakdown of heating or air conditioning can force last-minute cancellation or curtailment. Insurers are willing to indemnify against expenses and lost revenue from cancellation of a meeting or from continuation of it under adverse circumstances. This insurance should be considered.

- The holding of major meetings can give rise to special kinds and extraordinary amounts of potential liability for the organization conducting the meeting. Coverage for this extra liability in a comprehensive general liability insurance policy may be insufficient. Special high-policy-limit umbrella insurance for major meetings should be considered. Attention should also be paid to the possible need for special policies or riders in special circumstances such as if, for example, tours are to be given or events conducted via watercraft.

Chapter 30 Resources

Books

Foster. "Hotel Attrition Clauses." In *(1999) Legal Symposium*. Washington, D.C.: American Society of Association Executives, 1999.

Foster. "Event Contracts Update." In *(2001) Legal Symposium*. Washington, D.C.: American Society of Association Executives, 2002, p. 91.

Foster. "Event Contracts Update: What You Need to Know Now!" In *2002 DC Legal Symposium*. Washington, D.C.: American Society of Association Executives, 2002, p. 253.

Foster. "Drafting Contracts in Uncertain Times." In *2003 DC Legal Symposium*. Washington, D.C.: American Society of Association Executives, 2003, p. 175.

Foster. "Understanding and Reviewing Complex Contracts." In *2004 DC Association Law Symposium*. Washington, D.C.: American Society of Association Executives, 2004, p. 93

Foster. "Hotel Contract Damages: What's Legal—What's Appropriate?" In *2005 Annual Association Law Symposium*. Washington, D.C.: American Society of Association Executives, 2005, p. 361.

Foster. "Pitfalls to Avoid When Negotiating Convention Center Licenses." In *2005 Annual Association Law Symposium*. Washington, D.C.: American Society of Association Executives, 2005, p. 383.

Glassie. "Entering into Contracts Abroad." In *Conducting International Meetings*. Washington, D.C.: Greater Washington Society of Association Executives Foundation, 1993, p. 59.

Glassie. *International Legal Issues for Nonprofit Organizations*. Washington, D.C.: American Society of Association Executives, 1999, p. 177.

Glassie. "Hotel Contracts after 9/11." In *Associations and the Law*. Jacobs, ed. Washington, D.C.: American Society of Association Executives, 2002, p. 89.

Glassie. "Increasing Protection Against Attrition Penalties." In *Associations and the Law*. Jacobs, ed. Washington, D.C.: American Society of Association Executives, 2002, p. 91.

Glassie. "Expansion/Renovation Clauses in Hotel/Convention Center Contracts." In *Associations and the Law*. Jacobs, ed. Washington, D.C.: American Society of Association Executives, 2002, p. 93.

Glassie. "No Attrition Clause—Still an Attrition Obligation?" In *Associations and the Law*. Jacobs, ed. Washington, D.C.: American Society of Association Executives, 2002, p. 96.

Mandel and Goldberg. "Hotel Contracts: How to Increase Your Negotiating Muscle in a Seller's Market." In *(1996) Legal Symposium*. Washington, D.C.: American Society of Association Executives, 1996, p. 420.

Articles

Dunn. "Force Majeure Clauses for the 21st Century." *Association Law & Policy* (July 1, 2003).

Foster. "Defensive Hotel Contract Negotiation." *Association Law & Policy* (January, 2005).

Cases

Hyatt Corp. v. Women's International Bowling Congress, Inc., 80 F.Supp.2nd 88 (W.D.N.Y. 1999). Unsuccessful attempt by hotel to impose a noncontract attrition penalty on association.

Lederman Enterprises v. Allied Social Science Associations, 709 P.2d 1 (Colo.App. 1985). Appellate court found no basis for damages when hotel canceled contract, concluding the hotel had only agreed to make rooms available if nonprofit organization used the rooms.

National Ass'n. of Postmasters of the U.S. v. Hyatt Regency Washington, 894 A.2d 471 (D.C.App. 2006). Appellate court affirmed damages against association for canceling one year in advance of meeting when a government order required most members to be elsewhere, finding no "emergency" under *force majeur* clause.

Chapter 42
Political Action Committee Organization

The organization of an association-related political action committee (PAC) that will support candidates for election to federal office is dictated in many ways by stringent federal election laws. To maintain tax-exempt status and to achieve tax benefits for contributors, association-related PACs must observe even further federal requirements.

Summary

- Organization of association-related PACs is subject to several considerations dictated by federal laws, regulations, and Federal Election Commission (FEC) interpretations.

- The official name of the PAC must include the full name of the association sponsoring it. That full name must be included in the FEC statement of organization, on all reports, and as part of any legal notices required on solicitations. The FEC has advised that an abbreviated name for the PAC can be used on letterhead and checks of the PAC. For example, the National Widget Association (NWA) should name its PAC the National Widget Association Political Action Committee. On letterhead or checks, it may use a recognizable abbreviation, such as NWA PAC. It may not be satisfactory to name or call its PAC the Good Government Fund or Widget PAC.

- The law requires a PAC to be registered within 10 days following its formation and requires its registration to be updated within 10 days after information on the registration changes. The registration must use FEC Form 1, must be signed by the PAC's treasurer, and must include:

  - The name, address, e-mail address, Web page, and, for an existing PAC updating information, the FEC identification number for the PAC.

  - An explanation of the nature of the PAC as connected to another organization such as a trade association, membership organization, or other entity.

  - An indication of whether the PAC is a "Lobbyist/Registrant PAC" by virtue of its connected organization's registering as a lobbying organization (a 2009 FEC change per the Honest Leadership and Open Government Act).

- ◆ The name, address, and relationship of any connected organization.

- ◆ The name, address, and position of the custodian of the books and accounts of the PAC.

- ◆ The name and address of the treasurer of the PAC and of a designated agent such as an assistant treasurer.

- ◆ A listing of all banks, safety deposit boxes, and other depositories used by the PAC.

- A statement that the PAC's registration is filed with the FEC.

- The registration statement must be amended within 10 days whenever information given previously has changed. For example, whenever a new treasurer is appointed, the registration must be amended.

- Upon submitting its registration, the PAC will receive an identification number, which must be used on all filings.

- If it is intended that support will be given to state candidates as well as to federal candidates, it may be desirable to establish separate federal-level and state-level PACs and to register them individually. Complex expense allocation rules may apply if a PAC supports both federal and state candidates from separate federal and nonfederal accounts. Exclusively state-level PACs may be subject to different rules and do not have to be registered with the federal government.

- Association-related PACs need not be incorporated. In fact, federal law prohibits campaign contributions by corporations. FEC regulations do permit PACs to incorporate, but for liability purposes only. Notwithstanding this incorporation, however, treasurers of PACs remain personally responsible for their duties under the law.

- For the PAC to gain and maintain tax-exempt status, an IRS test is applied. The PAC must be organized and operated primarily to accept contributions and make expenditures intended to influence the selection, nomination, election, or appointment of individuals for public office. When a PAC meets this test, revenue received in the form of contributions is clearly exempt from federal income tax. The Internal Revenue Code and regulations for political committees detail what other kinds of PAC income qualify as exempt function income to avoid federal taxation. Interest received by a PAC on its deposited funds, for example, would not be exempt from taxation but would be subject to a $100 specific deduction.

- Charitable and other nonprofit organizations that are tax exempt under Section 501(c)(3) are prohibited from participating in any political activities and, therefore, from establishing or conducting any activities in connection with a PAC.

- A PAC must have a treasurer in office whenever funds are received or disbursed. The bylaws and registration statement therefore should provide for an assistant treasurer to serve if the treasurer is not available.

- Funds of the related association may be used to pay for PAC administrative and solicitation costs. Association funds cannot be used as contributions to the PAC or as contributions to candidates through the PAC. Examples of PAC administrative costs that can be paid from association funds—thereby maximizing the amount of PAC funds that can be used to make expenditures to political candidates—include

    - Printing, mailing, and other expenses for PAC solicitations.

    - Salaries of PAC employees or association employees assigned to PAC administrative activities.

    - Rent and other expenses of maintaining PAC offices.

    - Fees for attorneys, accountants, political consultants, direct mail consultants, or other professional advisers to the PAC.

- The related association's expenses for administering a PAC are considered lobbying expenses under the 1993 law disallowing federal income tax deductibility for association members' dues to the extent of the association's lobbying expenses. Thus the related association must include PAC administrative costs in its calculation of dues nondeductibility.

- It is clear that executives of a trade association's member companies may contribute their time to operating a PAC. However, corporations cannot deduct lobbying expenses for federal income tax purposes because of the same 1993 law that affects dues non-deductibility. So a trade association member company's expenses to have its executives volunteer to help operate the association-related PAC are also nondeductible.

Chapter 42 Resources

Books

Commerce Clearing House. *Federal Election Campaign Financing Guide.* Washington, D.C.: CCH.

Federal Election Commission. *Campaign Guide for Corporations and Labor Organizations.* Washington, D.C.: FEC, 2001.

Federal Election Commission. *BCRA Campaign Guide Supplement*, Washington, DC: FEC, 2003.

Statutes and Regulations

Bipartisan Campaign Reform Act of 2002, Public Law 107-155.

Internal Revenue Code, Section 501(c).

Internal Revenue Code, 527.

Internal Revenue Service TD 8602.

Internal Revenue Service Rev. Proc. 95-35.

Federal Election Campaign Act of 1971, as amended, 2 U.S.C. Sections 432, 433.

Federal Election Regulations, 11 C.F.R. Section 102 (19850); 11 C.F.R. Section 114.1(b) (1985).

Omnibus Budget Reconciliation Act of 1993, P.L. 103-66, Section 13222, 107 Stat. 312 (1993).

Treas. Reg. Sections 1.162-28, 29.

Other Resources

FEC Advisory Opinion 1980-10. Name of a PAC.

FEC Advisory Opinion 1980-23. Name of a PAC.

FEC Advisory Opinion 1980-59. Corporate member contribution to PAC to defray administration and solicitation costs.

FEC Advisory Opinion 1988-42. Name of a PAC.

FEC Advisory Opinion 1993-7. Name of a PAC.

FEC Form 1.

IRS Form 1120-POL.

IRS Technical Advice Memoranda 8202019 and 8202021 (1982).

Chapter 48
Congressional Gifts & Travel

Nonprofit organizations and associations often seek participation by congressional officials and executive branch employees at meetings or conventions. It is common to invite a member of Congress or an executive branch employee to speak at a convention or symposium; it is equally common to invite a member, congressional staffer, or executive branch employee to participate in a fact-finding trip or study mission to learn more about the industry, profession, or field of interest of the organization. Organizations may provide awards or plaques to congressional officials or executive branch employees. In the course of lobbying and political activities, representatives of associations may find themselves offering meals or other hospitality to members of Congress, congressional staff and officials, and employees of the executive branch. All of these activities actually are considered "gifts" to congressional and executive branch officials. In 1993, strict rules went into effect governing gifts that may be accepted by employees and officials of the executive branch. In 1996, strict rules went into effect governing gifts that may be accepted by members of the House of Representatives, the Senate, and employees of congressional offices. This chapter concerns those gift provisions; it also addresses limitations on honoraria.

Summary

- Restrictions on gifts that may be accepted by members, officers, and employees of the U.S. Congress, both the Senate and the House of Representatives, became effective in 1996. In 2007, the gift rules for both the House and Senate were amended with even stricter restrictions. These amendments were achieved through a combination of statutory changes by the Honest Leadership and Open Government Act and amendments to the House Rules by the House of Representatives. The burden of compliance with the gift rules, which heretofore fell only on members and employees of Congress, has now been expanded to include lobbyists, agents of foreign principals, and private entities that employ lobbyists or agents of foreign principals. Each chamber has its own rules, which are similar but not identical.

- Under the amended rules, both the House and Senate prohibit members, officers, and employees from accepting any gifts from lobbyists, foreign agents, and their employers ("restricted persons"). The old rules that prohibit members and employees from accepting a gift worth $50 or more and prohibit them from receiving from any one source in a given year gifts with a total value of $100 or more (thus, allowable gifts are those valued at $49.99 or less per occasion, and with a cumulative total of up to $99.99 per calendar year) still apply to nonrestricted persons. Any gift (including a meal) of $10 or more counts toward this total limit. There are exceptions for some items of nominal value, such as food or refreshments not offered as part of a meal, baseball caps, T-shirts, and promotional products from a representative's home state. These exceptions are applicable to restricted persons as well.

- The rules in both chambers exempt certain items, including free attendance at widely attended conventions and similar events in which the member participates in an official capacity. Both also exempt travel expenses to meetings that are related to official duties, although all travel must be preapproved by the appropriate Ethics Committee. Travel expenses may not be accepted at all, though, from a registered lobbyist or foreign agent and, if made, must be publicly disclosed. Recreation in the course of official travel is not exempted from the gift limitations, nor is there an exception for entertainment unless it is provided as an integral part of an event and to all attendees, regardless of their congressional employment.

- Both the House and Senate rules define "gift" as "any gratuity, favor, discount, entertainment, hospitality, loan, forbearance or other item having monetary value," including services, training, transportation, lodging, and meals.

- Any gift to a family member, or to an individual based on that individual's relationship to a member, officer, or employee of the House of Representatives or the Senate, counts as a gift to the member, officer, or employee if it is given with the knowledge and acquiescence of the member, officer, or employee and that person has reason to believe the gift was given because of the official position (with the exception that, if food or refreshment is provided at the same time and place to both a member, officer, or employee, and spouse or dependent, only the food or refreshment provided to the member, officer, or employee is treated as a gift).

- The gift restrictions do not apply to the following:

  ◆ Free attendance provided by the sponsor of a widely attended event, such as a convention, conference, symposium, forum, panel discussion, dinner, viewing, reception, or similar event if: (1) the member, officer, or employee is a speaker or panel participant presenting information related to Congress or matters before Congress, or is performing a ceremonial function appropriate to the participant's official position; or (2) attendance at the event is appropriate to the performance of the official duties of the member, officer, or employee. "Free attendance" includes waiver of all or part of a conference or other fee, local transportation, food or refreshments taken in a group setting with substantially all of the attendees, entertainment that is an integral part of the event, and instructional materials furnished to all attendees. An event will be widely attended if there is a reasonable expectation that at least 25 persons (other than members of Congress or staffers) will attend the event and the attendance is open to members from throughout a given industry or profession, or those in attendance represent a range of persons interested in a given matter.

◆ A sponsor's unsolicited offer of free attendance to a widely attended event for an accompanying individual. In the Senate, this attendance is excluded from the value limitations only if others in attendance will be similarly accompanied or if such attendance is appropriate to assist representation of the Senate.

◆ Employers of lobbyists and foreign agents may pay for travel and related expenses for members, officers, or employees if necessary to participate in a one-day meeting, speaking engagement, fact-finding trip, or similar event. Each Chamber's Ethics Committee may permit a second night's stay if it concludes that the additional expenses are practically required for the individual to take part in the one-day event. This is determined on a case-by-case basis.

  ◆ Lobbyists and foreign agents are prohibited from paying for any portion of the cost of a trip; from planning, organizing, requesting, or arranging a trip; and from accompanying a member, officer, or employee on a trip.

  ◆ The member, officer, or employee must obtain preapproval from the appropriate Ethics Committee, and the sponsor must provide written certification to the individual that the trip is not financed, planned, organized, requested, or arranged by a lobbyist or foreign agent and certify that the individual will not be accompanied by a lobbyist or foreign agent on any portion of the one-day trip.

  ◆ Under the House Rules, colleges and universities (even those which employ lobbyists or foreign agents) are not subject to the one-day travel prohibition. Under the Senate Rules, nonprofit organizations with Section 501(c) (3) federal income tax exemption status may provide travel for more than one-day with preapproval from the Ethics Committee.

- A private sponsor, other than a registered lobbyist, foreign agent, or entity that employs such individuals, may pay for necessary travel expenses for a member, officer, or employee to attend a multiple-day meeting, fact-finding trip, or similar event in connection with his or her official duties. Events of a substantially recreational nature are not considered to be in connection with official duties. The sponsor of the officially connected travel must provide a Private Source Form to each invitee and the member, employee, or official must obtain preapproval from the appropriate Ethics Committee.

- Travel expenses that are permitted under the rules are limited to those that are reasonable and necessary. Necessary expenses include reasonable expenses for transportation, food, and lodging, but do not include expenditures for entertainment or recreational activities. For each trip taken by a member, officer, or employee, a travel disclosure form must be completed, signed, and filed with the Clerk of the House within 15 days of return or with the Secretary of the Senate within 30 days of return.

- A sponsor's unsolicited offer of free attendance at a charity event for a member, officer, or employee, or a spouse or dependent. The invitation must come from the sponsoring charity itself. Corporations or other donors who underwrite the event are not considered "sponsors" for purposes of the gift rules. Transportation and lodging to a charity event may be accepted only under the Senate rule, and then only if the event meets the standards (discussed above) for meetings, speaking engagements, or similar events (for example, if the charity event is substantially recreational in nature, transportation and lodging may not be accepted).

- Anything for which the member, officer, or employee pays market value, or does not use and promptly returns.

- A lawful federal campaign contribution and, under the House rule, a lawful contribution for election to state or local office.

- Attendance at a fund-raising event sponsored by a political organization described in Section 527(e) of the Internal Revenue Code of 1986.

- A gift from a relative.

- Anything (expressly including personal hospitality under the Senate rule, even if provided by a registered lobbyist or an agent of a foreign principal) given by an individual on the basis of a personal friendship, unless the recipient has reason to believe that, under the circumstances, the gift was provided because of the official position of the recipient. In deciding whether the gift is on the basis of personal friendship, relevant circumstances include the history of the relationship between the donor and the recipient; whether, to the actual knowledge of the recipient, the donor personally paid for the gift or sought a tax deduction or business reimbursement for it; and whether, to the actual knowledge of the recipient, the donor gave similar gifts to other members, officers, or employees at the same time. For gifts valued at greater than $250, however, the Committee on Standards of Official Conduct (under the House rule) or the Senate Committee on Ethics (under the Senate rule) must issue a written determination that the "personal friendship" exception applies.

- A lawful contribution (by someone other than a registered lobbyist or an agent of a foreign principal) to a legal expense fund established for the benefit of the member, officer, or employee.

- Any gift from another member, officer, or employee of the Senate or the House of Representatives.

- Food, refreshments, lodging, and other benefits (such as transportation): (1) resulting from the outside business or other outside activities of the member, officer, or employee, or of that person's spouse, if the benefits have not been offered or enhanced because of that person's official position and are customarily provided to others; or (2) customarily provided by a prospective employer in connection with bona fide employment discussions; or (3) provided by a political organization described in Section 527(e) of the Internal Revenue Code of 1986 in connection with a fund-raising or campaign event sponsored by that organization.

- Pension and other benefits maintained by a former employer.

- Informational materials sent to the office, such as books, articles, periodicals, audiotapes, or videotapes.

- Awards or prizes that are given to competitors in contests or events open to the public.

- Honorary degrees (and associated travel, food, refreshments, and entertainment) and other bona fide, nonmonetary awards presented in recognition of public service (and associated food, refreshments, and entertainment provided in the presentation of the degrees and awards).

- Training (including food and refreshments furnished to all attendees as an integral part) if such training is in the interest of the House of Representatives or of the Senate.

- Bequests, inheritances, and other transfers at death.

- Any item authorized by the Foreign Gifts and Decorations Act, the Mutual Educational and Cultural Exchange Act, or any other statute.

- Anything paid for by the federal, state, or local government or secured under a government contract.

- A gift of personal hospitality by someone other than a registered lobbyist or agent of a foreign principal.

- Opportunities and benefits that are available to particular groups, specifically to: (1) the public or all federal employees; or (2) members of a group or class in which membership is unrelated to congressional employment; or (3) members of an organization in which membership is related to congressional employment if similar opportunities are available to large segments of the public through organizations of similar size; or (4) any group or class that is not defined in a manner that specifically discriminates among government employees on the basis of branch of government or type of responsibility, or that favors those of higher rank or pay; or (5) the public in the form of loans from banks and other financial institutions; or (6) all government employees in the form of reduced membership or other fees for participation in professional organization activities offered, if the only restrictions on membership relate to professional qualifications.

- A plaque, trophy, or other item that is substantially commemorative and intended solely for presentation.

- Anything for which a waiver is granted by the Committee on Standards of Official Conduct under the House rule or the Select Committee on Ethics under the Senate rule.

- Food or refreshments of nominal value offered as other than part of a meal.

- Donations of products from the state the member represents that primarily are intended for promotional purposes and are of minimal value to any individual recipient.

- An item of nominal value, such as a greeting card, baseball cap, or T-shirt.

- Under both the House and Senate rules, members, officers, or employees may not accept certain items from a registered lobbyist (i.e., the individual registered lobbyist) or an agent of a foreign principal regardless of their value. Those prohibited gifts include (1) anything provided to an entity controlled or maintained by the member, officer, or employee; (2) a contribution or other payment to a legal expense fund established for the benefit of the member, officer, or employee; and (3) a financial contribution or expenditure relating to a conference, retreat, or similar event sponsored by or affiliated with an official congressional organization, for or on behalf of members, officers, or employees.

- Charitable contributions by lobbyists and agents of foreign principals based on a designation, recommendation, or other specification by a member, officer, or employee also are prohibited unless made in lieu of an honorarium and the member, officer, or employee reports within 30 days the designation, the name and address of the lobbyist and the charitable organization, and the date and amount of the contribution to the Clerk of the House of Representatives under the House rule or to the Secretary of the Senate under the Senate rule. The Clerk and Secretary, respectively, are to make public this information as soon as possible.

- An honorarium is the payment of money or anything else of value that is to be paid to an elected or appointed officer or employee of the federal government in return for an appearance, speech, or article by the official. Honoraria can no longer be paid to members of Congress or staffers, but they may designate a charitable organization to receive the payment (limited to $2,000), and it will then not be considered a prohibited honorarium.

- Employees of the executive branch are regulated by the Office of Government Ethics, Standards of Ethical Conduct for Employees of the executive branch (the "OGE rules"). In addition, many agencies have adopted their own Supplemental Standards of Ethical Conduct.

    - The OGE rules provide that an employee may not, directly or indirectly, solicit or accept a gift from a prohibited source or a gift that is given because of the employee's official position.

    - The OGE rules define a "gift" as any gratuity, favor, discount, entertainment, hospitality, loan, or other item having monetary value, including services as well as transportation, lodgings, and meals. Relevant items not included are:

        - Modest items of food and refreshments, such as soft drinks, coffee, and donuts, offered other than as part of a meal; greeting cards and items with little intrinsic value, such as plaques, certificates, and trophies, which are intended solely for presentation; opportunities and benefits, including favorable rates and commercial discounts, available to the public or to a class consisting of all government employees or all uniformed military personnel, whether or not restricted on the basis of geographic considerations.

- ◆ The OGE rules define a "prohibited source" to include "any person who: (1) is seeking official action by the employee's agency; (2) does business or seeks to do business with the employee's agency; (3) conducts activities regulated by the employee's agency; (4) has interests that may be substantially affected by performance or nonperformance of the employee's official duties; or 5) is an organization a majority of whose members are described in paragraphs (1) through (4)."

- ◆ The OGE gift restrictions do not apply to the following: gifts based on personal friendship; benefits customarily provided by a prospective employer in connection with bona fide employment discussions widely attended gatherings; gifts provided subject to the $20/$50 exception (this includes gifts with a value of under $20 per source per occasion, but no more than $50 per year from that source. Buy-downs are not permitted.); benefits resulting from outside business/employment of spouse; food and entertainment when on duty or official travel in a foreign area; gifts provided as part of a bona fide "award or honorary degree;" social invitations from persons other than prohibited sources; discounts and similar benefits (may accept reduced membership fees in a professional organization if the discount is offered to all government employees with the appropriate professional qualifications); gifts in connection with political activities permitted by the Hatch Act Reform Amendments.

- ◆ On January 21, 2009, President Obama signed an executive order entitled "Executive Commitments by Executive Branch Personnel." The Order requires appointees, appointed on or after January 20, 2009, to commit (by signing a Lobbyist Gift Ban Pledge) to not accept gifts or gratuities from lobbyists or lobbying organizations (Registrants). It also expands the revolving-door rules and requires appointees to sign a Pledge that they will abide by the rules.

  - ◆ The Order adopts the definition of "gift" as provided in the OGE rules. "Appointee" includes "every full time, non career Presidential or Vice-Presidential appointee, non career appointee in the Senior Executive Service (or other SES type system), and appointee to a position that has been exempted from the competitive service by reason of being of a confidential or policymaking character (Schedule C and other positions exempted under comparable criteria) in an executive agency. It does not include any person appointed as a member of the Senior Foreign Service or solely as a uniformed service commissioned officer."

◆ The Order eliminates some of the very old exceptions that are listed above. Political appointees cannot accept: gifts provided subject to the $20/$50 exception; free attendance at "widely attended gatherings"; food and entertainment when on duty or official travel in a foreign area; gifts provided as part of a bona fide "award or honorary degree"; social invitations from persons other than prohibited sources; gifts in connection with political activities permitted by the Hatch Act Reform Amendments.

Chapter 48 Resources

Books
Bonvillian. "Lobbying and Ethics of Federal Officials." In *Federal Lobbying Law Handbook, 2d ed*. Jacobs, ed. Washington, D.C.: American Society of Association Executives, 1993, p. 38.

Statutes and Regulations
House of Representatives Rule XXV.
Senate Rule XXXV.
Ethics Reform Act of 1989, Pub. L. No. 101-194, Nov. 30, 1989.
Federal Election Campaign Act, 2 U.S.C. Section 441i.
Federal Election Regulations, 11 C.F.R.106.3.
Code of Federal Regulations, 5 C.F.R. 2635.202-2635.204

Other Resources
House of Representatives, Committee on Standards of Official Conduct, Memorandum on New Gift Rule, Dec. 7, 1995.
House of Representatives, Committee on Standards of Official Conduct, Memorandum on Widely Attended and Other Events under the New Gift Rule, Mar. 18, 1996.
Senate Select Committee on Ethics, Senate Ethics Manual (2003).
House Committee on Standards of Official Conduct, Gift and Travel Booklet (2000).
Executive Order 13490, Ethics Commitments by Executive Branch Personnel, January 21, 2009.

Chapter 49
Lobbying Registration & Reporting

The Lobbying Disclosure Act of 1995 replaced the Federal Regulation of Lobbying Act of 1946, which had governed federal-level registration and disclosure by lobbyists for 50 years. The effectiveness of the 1946 statute had been severely limited by federal court decisions. The 1995 act was designed to avoid similar problems while broadening registration and disclosure requirements. In 2007, the United States Congress further enhanced and expanded the law of federal lobbying registration and reporting when it enacted the Honest Leadership and Open Government Act. The law requires an organization that lobbies, such as an association, corporation, or consulting firm, to register with the Senate and House. Associations and corporations register for the in-house lobbyists employed within their organizations; consulting firms register for each lobbying client that engages the firms (thus relieving their clients of the obligation if the clients do no more than very modest amounts of in-house lobbying). Organizations that register also must file quarterly reports describing their lobbying activities; particularly what matters are the subjects of their lobbying and how much is spent on the lobbying. Compliance with the laws is relatively straightforward; noncompliance can result in serious criminal and civil penalties. Accordingly, associations and other nonprofit organizations that engage in any federal-level lobbying should pay careful attention to the law and comply scrupulously with its requirements.

Summary

- The Lobbying Disclosure Act of 1995 requires registration by every lobbyist at the federal level.

  - A "lobbyist" is a person or firm "employed or retained by a client for financial or other compensation" to make more than one "lobbying contact," including a lobbyist employed in-house by an association.

  - For associations that employ lobbyists (as with business corporations), the association files the registration on behalf of all of its employed lobbyists. For a consulting firm that includes lobbyists (such as a law firm or lobbying firm), the firm files a separate registration for each lobbying client.

  - When in a three-month period the lobbying activities of an association's employed lobbyist amount to less than 20 percent of the overall time spent working for the association employer, or the lobbying activities for a consulting firm's client amount to less than 20 percent of the time spent working for the consulting firm's client, the association employee or the consulting firm is not considered a "lobbyist" for that association or client, respectively.

◆ An association that has employees lobbying in-house on its own behalf and has total lobbying expenses under $11,500 in a three-month reporting period, or a consulting firm with lobbying income from a client under $3,000 in the three-month period, need not register as an association or for that client, respectively. These dollar thresholds are subject to Consumer Product Index adjustments every four years.

• A "lobbying contact" is any oral or written communication made on behalf of an employer or client to a "covered legislative or executive branch official" regarding any of several subjects. A "lobbying activity" is any action taken in support of a lobbying contact, including planning and preparation, research intended for use in the contact, and coordination with other lobbyists.

◆ The law covers lobbying the executive branch at certain levels as well as lobbying the U.S. Congress. Covered officials include not only members of Congress and cabinet secretaries but also staffers, aides, and many other employees.

◆ Subjects of lobbying contacts include the formulation, modification, or adoption of federal legislation, including legislative proposals, or of executive branch policies, including rules, regulations, and executive orders; the administration or execution of a federal program or policy; and the nomination or confirmation of any person who requires Senate confirmation.

• The law specifies certain types of communications that are not considered "lobbying contacts." Exceptions that may be relevant for associations include:

◆ communications published or disseminated to the public

◆ communications made on behalf of foreign governments or political parties (which remain covered by the Foreign Agents Registration Act)

◆ communications that the communicator could not report without disclosing information illegally

-◆ communications that the government is legally required to keep confidential

◆ administrative requests for information

    ◆ participation in a federal advisory committee

    ◆ testimony before a committee or subcommittee of Congress

    ◆ written responses to a covered official's request for specific information

    ◆ legally compelled communications, such as responses to subpoenas

    ◆ comments responsive to notices of proposed rulemaking

    ◆ statements made in the course of judicial or administrative adjudications

    ◆ requests for agency action on the public record

    ◆ any communications made on the record in public proceedings

• The law does not cover grassroots lobbying, such as campaigns to solicit public letter writing or phone calling to influence policy decisions.

• Within 45 days of the date the lobbyist first makes a lobbying contact for the employer association or for a consulting firm's client, or within 45 days of the date a lobbyist is engaged to make a lobbying contact—whichever happens earlier—the lobbyist must register with the Secretary of the Senate and the Clerk of the House of Representatives. An association that has an employee who lobbies to a sufficient extent to trigger the law must file an association registration covering the association's in-house lobbyist; a consulting firm that has lobbyists who lobby for separate clients must file a registration for each client. A registration may be terminated by an association that ceases lobbying altogether or by a consulting firm that ceases lobbying for a client. Each registration must include:

    ◆ The name, address of the principal place of business, and business telephone number of the registrant association (or the registrant firm and client), including a general description of its business or activities.

    ◆ The name, address, and principal place of business of any organization that contributes more than $5,000 in the three-month reporting period toward the registrant's lobbying activities and actively participates in the planning, supervision, or control of the lobbying activities.

    ◆ The name, address, and principal place of business of any foreign entity that has significant ties either to a controlling organization or to an organization for which lobbying is conducted, the amount of any contribution over $5,000 the foreign entity has made to the registrant's lobbying activities, and the approximate percentage of any equitable ownership the foreign entity holds in the organization for which lobbying is conducted.

- ◆ A statement of the general issue areas about which the registrant expects to lobby and any specific issues the registrant's lobbying activities have already addressed or are likely to address.

- ◆ The name of any lobbyist the registration covers who, in the 20 years before the lobbyist first lobbied on behalf of the organization for which lobbying is conducted, served as a covered legislative or executive branch official, and the position that lobbyist held when in the federal government.

- After the initial registration, an association that employs lobbyists, or an outside lobbying firm, must electronically file with the Secretary and the Clerk quarterly disclosure reports. The due dates for each quarterly report, commencing on January 1 and each subsequent three-month period thereafter, are April 20, July 20, October 20, and January 20. Each report must include:

  - ◆ Any changes to the information in the initial registration.

  - ◆ With respect to each general issue area in which the registrant lobbied during the reporting period, a list of specific issues on which the registrant engaged in lobbying activities, including, where practicable, specific bill numbers and references to executive branch actions; which Houses of Congress and executive agencies the registrant or its employed lobbyists contacted; a list of employees of the registrant who were lobbyists on behalf of the organization for which lobbying is conducted; and a description of any interest any foreign entity listed in the registration had in the specific issues on which the registrant lobbied.

  - ◆ A good-faith estimate of the registrant's total income during the reporting period for lobbying activities on the client's behalf where the report is made by a consulting firm or, in the case of a registrant such as an association lobbying on its own behalf, a good-faith estimate of the registrant's total lobbying expenses.

  - ◆ Certain associations and other tax-exempt organizations required to calculate lobbying expenditures for tax-exemption purposes may use the relevant Internal Revenue Code definitions and calculations in their lobbying registration and reporting. This provision is intended to eliminate the need for exempt organizations to maintain two sets of books to keep track of lobbying expenses separately for tax-exemption and federal lobbying reporting purposes. It is clear that, although the definitions and calculations of lobbying expenses for tax-exemption purposes can be quite different than those for federal lobbying reporting purposes, the tax-exemption definitions and calculations may be used for this feature of federal lobbying reporting—the estimate of lobbying expenses during the reporting period.

- In addition to filing quarterly disclosure reports, every registered association and each active lobbyist is required to file a semi-annual contribution report disclosing specific payments made and certifying that no improper gifts have been made. This report is required regardless of whether there is any activity. The report must include:

  - The date, recipient, and amount of contributions of $200 or more made to any federal candidate or officeholder, leadership PAC, or political party committee (registered with the Federal Election Commission). This includes contributions made by an association's connected PAC.

  - The date, the name of honoree, the payee(s), and amount of funds $200 or more paid to each presidential library foundation and each presidential inaugural committee.

  - The date, recipient, and amount of funds contributed or disbursed:

    - To pay the cost of an event to "honor or recognize" a covered federal legislative or executive branch official. An official is "honored or recognized" if given a special award, recognition, or honor at the event. Speaking at the event does not form the basis for concluding that the official is to be honored or recognized

    - To an entity that is named for a covered federal legislative branch official, or to a person or entity in recognition of the official

    - To an entity established, financed, maintained, or controlled by a covered federal legislative or executive branch official, or an entity designated by the official

    - To pay the costs of a meeting, retreat, conference, or other similar event held by, or in the name of, one or more covered federal legislative or executive branch officials to discuss advocacy positions taken by the association

  - The form also requires a certification that the filer has read and understands the gift and travel provisions in the rules of both the House and the Senate, and that the filer has not knowingly violated those rules.

- In 2009, the Federal Election Commission implemented regulations for disclosure of lobbyist-bundled contributions to candidates for federal office that have special ramifications for organizations or individuals that are registered as lobbyists. The FEC lobbyist bundling disclosure rule requires "reporting committees," which include only authorized committees of federal candidates, leadership PACs, and political party committees, but not association-related PACs, to file bundling disclosure reports if they receive two or more bundled contributions exceeding $16,000 during the covered time period from a lobbyist (or lobbyist/registrant PAC committee).

  - As a result of the lobbyist bundling disclosure requirement, lobbyist/registrant PACs must identify themselves as such on their Statement of Organization (FEC Form 1).

  - A "lobbyist/registrant PAC" is a federal PAC with a current federal lobbying registrant filing federal lobbying reports with the Clerk of the House and the Secretary of the Senate, such as an association that registers because it employs in-house lobbyists, as its connected organization.

- The Secretary of the Senate and the Clerk of the House have initial responsibility for enforcement and public information under the law.

  - The Secretary and Clerk notify in writing any lobbyist or lobbying firm that may be in noncompliance with the law. If the association or firm does not provide an appropriate response within 60 days, the Secretary and the Clerk will inform the U.S. Attorney for the District of Columbia. Any person who fails to comply with any provision of the law is subject to a civil fine of up to $200,000. And especially daunting is that the law, as amended in 2007, contains criminal penalties for knowing and corrupt violations.

  - The Secretary and the Clerk maintain a publicly available list of all registered lobbyists, lobbying firms, and lobbying clients; make registrations and reports available for public inspection and copying; and retain registrations for six years after they are terminated and reports for six years after they are filed.

- The law contains several notable provisions not directly related to registration or reporting by lobbyists.

  - Any person making an oral lobbying contact with a covered official must, on request, tell the official whether the person is a registered lobbyist, which client the person is representing, whether that client is a foreign entity, and the identity of any foreign entity listed in the person's lobby registration with a direct interest in the outcome of the lobbying activity.

◆ Any registered lobbyist making a written lobbying contact with a covered official must likewise identify any foreign entity listed in the lobby registration with a direct interest in the outcome of the lobbying activity. In addition, if the client is a foreign entity, the lobbyist making a written contact must identify the client as such and state whether the lobbyist is registered under the law as a lobbyist for that client.

◆ Covered officials must, on request, identify themselves as such to anyone making a lobbying contact.

◆ Federal funding is prohibited for any organization tax exempt under Section 501(c)(4) of the Internal Revenue Code that engages in lobbying activities.

◆ Foreign entities, except foreign governments or political parties, are exempt from the registration requirement of the Foreign Agents Registration Act if those agents have registered as lobbyists. The law also lightens the Foreign Agents Registration Act's reporting requirements for agents of foreign entities when they transmit informational materials on behalf of their clients.

◆ The disclosure provisions of the Byrd Amendment, 31 U.S.C. Section 1352(B), which requires recipients of federal funding to disclose lobbying efforts used to secure that funding, are altered to conform with the registration and reporting requirements of the law.

Chapter 49 Resources

Books

Broadley. "Lobbying for Foreign Interests." In *Federal Lobbying Law Handbook, 2d ed.* Jacobs, ed. Washington, D.C.: American Society of Association Executives, 1993, p. 12.

Jacobs and Handzo. "Lobbying Registration." In *Federal Lobbying Law Handbook, 2d ed.* Jacobs, ed. Washington, D.C.: American Society of Association Executives, 1993, p. 1.

Articles

Altman and Henson. "Unresolved Issues Regarding the Lobbying Disclosure." *Association Law & Policy* (March 1, 1996): 5.

Ballentine. "The Lobbying Disclosure Act of 1995: Interpretation, Guidance and Remaining Issues." *Association Law & Policy* (August, 1997): 5.

Goldberg. "New Lobby Disclosure Law Changes the Rules for Association Lobbyists." *Association Law & Policy* (January 1, 1996): 5.

Statutes

Lobbying Disclosure Act of 1995, Pub. L. No. 104-65, Dec. 19, 1995, codified at 2 U.S.C. Section 1601 *et seq.*

Other Resources

Notice from the Secretary of the Senate and the Clerk of the House of Representatives, 141 Congressional Record H 15634, Dec. 22, 1995.

Lobbying Disclosure Act of 1995, H.R. Rep. No. 104-339(I), Nov. 14, 1995.

"Introduction: New Rules for Lobbyists and Lawmakers." Bureau of National Affairs Special Report, 1996.

Form LD-1, Lobbying Registration Form and Instructions.

Lobbying Disclosure Act Guidance, updated Feb. 3, 2009.

Chapter 51
Discussions at Meetings

Discussions at meetings of associations and other business or professional organizations often cover broad ranges of issues pertinent to the interests or concerns of participants. As a general rule, discussions can address any subject without raising antitrust concerns if the discussions are kept scrupulously free of even the suggestion of private regulation of an industry, profession, or field of endeavor. Participants should be aware that opinions expressed or conclusions reached at these meetings can never be binding on the participants. The opinions or conclusions are no more than informative presentations on which participants may act as each considers appropriate. A participant should always have the right to object to the discussion of any subject that might present legal problems. The advice of legal counsel can then be obtained. Some subjects clearly are not appropriate for discussion; others very likely are appropriate. A few of each are listed here.

A number of policies or programs that might be discussed at meetings raise issues of antitrust and trade regulation that are complex and have long series of court and agency decisions and opinions relating to them. These areas include membership restrictions, categories, and termination; membership services to nonmembers; trade show or advertising restrictions; business or professional codes of ethics; statistical surveys; price and fee activities; cost programs; standards development; product certification; program or entity accreditation; professional certification; joint research; credit reporting; group buying and selling; and others. Each of these has a separate summary on antitrust implications in succeeding chapters.

Summary

- Participants at association and other business or professional organization meetings, whether they be meetings of the membership, the governing board, officers, committees, or subcommittees, must be made aware that discussions of certain subjects raise grave antitrust dangers and therefore must be avoided.

- From a negative point of view, and in very general terms, there must be no discussions at meetings that may in any way tend to

  - Raise, lower, or stabilize prices or fees

  - Regulate production levels or schedules

  - Affect the availability of products or services

  - Affect allocation of markets, territories, customers, or patients

  - Encourage boycotts or exclusions of products or services

- Foster unfair practices involving advertising, merchandising, standardization, certification, or accreditation

- Encourage anyone to refrain from competing

- Limit or exclude anyone from manufacture, sale, or practice

- Result in illegal brokerage or rebates

- Affect improper reciprocity in dealing

- There are some topics of discussion that are best avoided at meetings:

  - Current or future prices (great care must be taken in discussing past prices)

  - What constitutes a fair profit or margin level

  - Possible increases or decreases in prices

  - Standardization or stabilization of prices

  - Pricing procedures

  - Cash discounts

  - Credit terms

  - Control of sales

  - Allocation of markets

  - Refusal to deal with a firm because of its pricing or distribution practices

  - Whether or not the pricing practices of any industry member are unethical or constitute an unfair trade practice

- Another commentator on antitrust compliance suggests a list of subjects that ordinarily should be avoided in discussions with competitors (e.g., at association and nonprofit organization meetings) lest an understanding or agreement on the subjects, expressed or implied, be effected and subsequently challenged:

  - Prices

  - Costs

  - Profits

  - Product or service offerings

  - Terms or conditions of sale

  - Deliveries

  - Production facilities or capacity

- ◆ Production or sales volume

- ◆ Market share

- ◆ Decisions to quote or not to quote

- ◆ Customer or supplier classification, allocation, or selection

- ◆ Sales territories

- ◆ Distribution methods or channels

- Clearly these commentators are taking a conservative view on what can be discussed at meetings without violating the law. In fact, the antitrust laws prohibit anticompetitive joint action, not just discussions with competitors. But most organizations take the prudent approach of avoiding any discussions among competitors at meetings or events that could lead to illegal joint action by the competitors lest the sponsoring organization be then implicated in illegal conduct.

- In 2009 the Federal Trade Commission (FTC) reached a settlement with a trade association in a case (*National Association of Music Merchants*) in which the members had regularly shared information about their prices and business strategies. What is notable about the proceeding is that the FTC did not allege that the association or its members actually violated the antitrust laws. Instead the FTC said the information exchanges lacked procompetitive justification and "had the purpose, tendency, and capacity to facilitate price coordination and collusion among competitors." The settlement requires the respondent association to implement an extremely rigorous antitrust compliance program

- From a positive point of view, ordinarily there can be appropriate discussions at meetings that have as a purpose or result

- ◆ Reporting on general industry or profession economic trends.

- ◆ Describing advances or problems in relevant technology or research.

- ◆ Demonstrating methods by which an individual or firm can become more profitable by acquiring better knowledge of its own costs.

- ◆ Summarizing effective methods of purchasing, manufacturing, and marketing.

- ◆ Educating about various aspects of the science and art of management.

- Considering trade industry or profession relations with local, state, or federal governments.

- Reporting on experiences and developments in employment relations.

- Relating efforts toward improvement of products.

- Developing ways to respond to consumer or environmental issues.

- Affecting energy use and supply.

- These very general lists of appropriate and inappropriate discussion goals or subjects are far from exhaustive or unequivocal. An area quite appropriate for discussion can be rendered inappropriate by an improper approach to it. The lists are illustrative only.

- If any area of legal concerns justifies constant and intense monitoring by legal counsel experienced in antitrust implications of association and other nonprofit organization policies and programs, it is the area of meeting discussions. The ramifications of antitrust laws and trade regulations are subtle and dynamic. They are not necessarily avoided merely by avoiding discussions in areas indicated in this summary. By all means, organizations should seek expert advice on the appropriateness of meeting discussions whenever questions are raised. Some invite counsel to attend all meetings of the governing boards or other bodies at which improper or illegal subjects could arise. Others have counsel review agendas and minutes for meetings. At the very least, counsel should be available to guide and assist on what are appropriate and inappropriate subjects for discussions at meetings.

Chapter 51 Resources

Books
Jacobs and Ogden. *Legal Risk Management for Associations.* Washington, D.C.: American Psychological Association, 1995, p. 107.

Other Resources
FTC Advisory Opinion 85, 70 F.T.C. 1867 (1967). Association information exchange regarding suppliers' products.
FTC Advisory Opinion 133, 72 F.T.C. 1037 (1967). Discussions among members on compliance with law.
FTC Advisory Opinion 137, 72 F.T.C. 1042 (1967). Discussions on firm pricing by suppliers.

FTC Advisory Opinion 407, 77 F.T.C. 1702 (1970). Discussion of voluntary standards.

FTC Advisory Opinion 475, 80 F.T.C. 1049 (1972). Information exchange on members' experience with equipment.

Cases

In the Matter of National Association of Music Merchants, Inc. File No. 001 0203, April 8, 2009.

Chapter 71
Antitrust Compliance Program

Because they are vehicles for bringing competitors together and conduits for moving information among competitors, many kinds of nonprofit organizations—especially trade associations and professional societies—are closely scrutinized for violations of the antitrust laws. This unique exposure to antitrust scrutiny dictates that these organizations should take steps to minimize the danger of becoming involved in antitrust investigations or litigation.

The immense complexity of the various and often overlapping antitrust laws precludes finding any administrative policies or procedures that could absolutely guarantee immunity from antitrust scrutiny. The Supreme Court's *Hydrolevel* decision even suggests a kind of "strict liability" of nonprofits for anticompetitive conduct of their representatives, real or apparent. Nevertheless, the prospect of antitrust investigations or litigation is so unattractive that organizations should take extraordinary measures to at least minimize their exposure.

Involvement in an antitrust investigation or lawsuit is singularly distasteful. Usually it is embarrassing. If a criminal antitrust case is lost, significant fines and jail terms are likely to be imposed. On occasion, trade associations have been ordered to be disbanded. Even if an antitrust case is won, the demands on the time of those involved can be enormous; legal fees and costs can accumulate to six or even seven figures.

One way for an organization to help avoid antitrust investigations or litigation is to institute an antitrust compliance program. This chapter outlines general features of these programs. Of course, the nature of the organization and its members will dictate the policies or procedures to be emphasized for each entity's compliance program.

Summary

- An antitrust compliance program is one way for a nonprofit to minimize its exposure to antitrust investigations or lawsuits. Compliance programs can be adopted for use by organizations of any size or kind. Those that are most exposed to antitrust risk are trade associations and professional societies.

- The central feature of an antitrust compliance program is the establishment of a formal policy against antitrust violations. The policy should

  ◆ Be written in strong but clear language.

  ◆ Contain detailed prohibitions in areas where the organization may have special concerns based on past experience or on the nature of the organization or its members.

- ◆ Be approved by the governing body.

- ◆ Be circulated widely among staff, officers, directors, and members.

- An antitrust policy can be inserted in the bylaws or can be adopted by resolution of the membership or governing body.

- Staff, officers, directors, and members should be provided with sufficient knowledge of the antitrust laws to be able to recognize antitrust problems when they arise. Employed executives in particular should take a definite interest in antitrust compliance and make review of potential areas of antitrust problems a part of regular procedure.

- Legal counsel experienced in antitrust matters should be readily available to answer any inquiries about situations that may have antitrust consequences. Familiarity between antitrust counsel and the organization, plus a flexible arrangement for legal fees, can best encourage necessary communication in this area. Legal counsel should be asked to briefly review recent antitrust developments from time to time for the benefit of staff, officers, directors, and members.

- Certain activities require nearly continuous staff scrutiny and participation by legal counsel in planning, effectuation, and reporting. Examples include price or fee activities, cost programs, codes of ethics, standards development, and certification of professionals.

- Records—both paper and electronic—should be maintained in a way that ensures the records reflect factual, objective, and businesslike accounts of activities without useless or outdated information. A record retention program should be instituted to ensure that only necessary materials are kept. Such items as noncurrent documents, penciled notes, and document drafts usually have insignificant lasting value and should be regularly discarded. Once an investigation or lawsuit is pending or even threatened, destruction of documents is likely subject to legal prohibitions.

- No antitrust compliance program can be effective unless all those who deal with the organization are kept aware of potential antitrust dangers. Antitrust investigations or lawsuits usually can be avoided if those dealing with the organization know the rules and are motivated to follow them.

- Attention needs to be given, in antitrust compliance, not only to the main organization but also to all subsidiaries, affiliates, and chapters. Antitrust problems for national organizations often have arisen in these related organizations. There is at least one case indicating that an organization cannot be found to have conspired with its chartered local chapter on the principle that the two operate so closely together that they should not be considered separate entities (*Jack Russell Terrier Network* case); however, that principle may not always apply in situations in which related groups are accused of violating the antitrust laws by conspiring with one another.

- A sample antitrust compliance program might include the following features:

  - The program can be referenced, summarized, or set out in the bylaws, with a full account and procedures carefully detailed in some other document.

  - A strong and clear statement of the organization's continuing and undeviating policy to comply strictly with the letter and spirit of all federal, state, and applicable international trade regulations and antitrust laws is the heart of the compliance program.

  - Procedures for conducting all meetings pursuant to agendas distributed in advance, limitation of meeting discussions to agenda items, and prompt distribution of minutes to attendees should be followed.

  - Specific prohibitions should be included against activities or discussions that could be construed as tending to (1) raise, lower, or stabilize prices or fees; (2) regulate production or the availability of services; (3) allocate markets, customers, clients, or patients; (4) encourage boycotts; (5) foster unfair practices; (6) assist monopolization or in any way violate antitrust laws and trade regulations.

  - Provisions should be made for counsel to attend certain designated meetings routinely and to attend other meetings when the meeting subjects make it appropriate.

- In 2009 the Federal Trade Commission (FTC) reached a settlement with a trade association in a case *(National Association of Music Merchants)* in which the members had regularly shared information about their prices and business strategies. What is notable about the proceeding is that FTC did not allege that the association or its members actually violated the antitrust laws. Instead FTC said the information exchanges lacked procompetitive justification and "had the purpose, tendency, and capacity to facilitate price coordination and collusion among competitors." The settlement requires the respondent association to implement an extremely rigorous antitrust compliance program that would include:

- ◆ Review by the association's antitrust counsel of all written materials and prepared remarks by any member of the association's board of directors, or any employee or agent of the association relating to members' price terms;

- ◆ Provision by antitrust counsel of appropriate guidance on compliance with the antitrust laws; and

- ◆ Annual training of the association's board of directors, agents, and employees concerning the association's obligations.

- These and other, similar features of this singular FTC settlement might be more than is necessary in many associations and other nonprofit organizations; however, the settlement provides strong evidence of what the federal government thinks is required in situations where antitrust risks are rife.

Chapter 71 Resources

Books

ABA Section of Antitrust Law. *Antitrust and Associations Handbook* (2009).

Jacobs and Ogden. *Legal Risk Management for Associations.* Washington, D.C.: American Psychological Association, 1995, p. 23.

Portman. "Association Antitrust; Association Antitrust Compliance Policy; Medical Society Antitrust Compliance Policy," In *2005 Annual Association Law Symposium.* Washington, D.C.: American Society of Association Executives, 2005, p. 35.

Cases

In the Matter of National Association of Music Merchants, Inc. File No. 001 0203, April 8, 2009.

Jack Russell Terrier Network v. Am. Kennel Club, Inc., 407 F.3d 1027 (9th Cir. 2005). National association and its local chartered chapter found not to be subject to an antitrust conspiracy accusation based on the relatedness of the two organizations.

Chapter 81
For-Profit Subsidiaries

Until recently, trade, professional, and similar associations had become identified with a handful of conventional programs intended to enhance and advance the industries, professions, or fields they represented: conventions, trade shows, exhibitions, seminars, and other educational meetings; journals, newsletters, manuals, and all sorts of educational publications; public affairs initiatives to influence the government and the public; product and professional standards and certification; joint statistical gathering; labor negotiations; research and testing; and marketing, promotion, and advertising.

Likewise, social welfare or "cause" organizations—as well as charitable, educational, scientific, and similar organizations—had also become identified with conventional programs intended to enhance and advance their causes, missions, or goals pursued: health, education, research, fundraising, publications, journals, and so on.

Associations and other exempt organizations still do all those things, and they do them bigger and better than ever. But endeavors of exempt organizations are no longer limited to the conventional. They are expanding beyond their traditional roles and predictable activities to further their missions. The accent is on service using whatever creative and innovative policies and programs, within the law, work best. A secondary but important consideration is generating new forms of revenue, because many organizations have already tapped traditional sources—dues, donations, and so on—to their maximum without fulfilling all the needs and expectations of members, donors, or other constituencies. Funding new opportunities and new sources of revenue sometimes requires going beyond what's "always been done."

Inevitably, associations and other exempt organizations are turning more and more to establishing owned and controlled subsidiaries as the organizational entities from which to operate these creative or innovative programs to service constituencies. There are two major reasons for using subsidiaries.

First, as new programs approach the fringes of what has been determined as the appropriate scope of endeavor for a federal income tax–exempt organization, or even move beyond those fringes, the establishment of a separate subsidiary is necessary to protect and preserve the exempt status of the main organization. A tax-exempt organization can conduct unrelated business activities within the organization as long as the income from them is modest compared with that from other exemption-related activities. But as the income from the programs grows, it risks endangering the exempt status of the organization. Moving unrelated programs to a separate subsidiary removes this risk to exemption.

Second, some of the new endeavors may raise additional or different issues of legal liability exposure than that which the main organization has long experienced. It is therefore often best to limit that exposure if possible to the assets of a separately incorporated subsidiary.

This chapter considers tax-exemption and liability aspects of owned and controlled for-profit taxable subsidiaries.

Summary

- The most common use of an association or exempt organization subsidiary is to avoid tainting the federal income tax–exempt status of the main organization. A subsidiary established for this purpose is usually a for-profit (not tax-exempt) corporation equivalent to any incorporated taxpaying business, in this case one that is owned and controlled by the parent exempt organization.

- For-profit subsidiaries are ordinarily essential for conducting business activities that are clearly and obviously unrelated to the purposes for which an organization holds tax-exempt status and are likely to generate substantial net revenues—for example, an actively promoted insurance program, fee-for-service consulting, a publication outside the organization's field, and so forth.

- The main categories of federal income tax exemption available under the Internal Revenue Code ("IRC") to nonprofit business, professional, membership, charitable, and cause organizations are these:

  - IRC Section 501(c)(3). These are educational, religious, charitable, scientific, literary, or amateur sports organizations. This category offers the singular opportunity among those addressed here for donations to the organizations to be eligible for charitable federal income tax deductibility by the donors beyond the value of anything the donors receive in return for their donations. These organizations are subject to an "exclusivity" test; they must be organized and operated exclusively to advance their tax-exempt purposes. They must completely avoid political campaign activity. They must avoid engaging in "substantial" lobbying activities at the federal, state, or local levels [but have available an alternative mathematical test under IRC Section 501(h) as the measure of permissible lobbying]. They are subject to penalties under IRC Section 4958 if they provide "excess benefits," that is, above-market-value payments, to "insiders" (called "disqualified persons"). They are subject to a vague "commerciality" doctrine apparently prohibiting overtly or excessively commercial undertakings.

  - IRC Section 501(c)(4). These are social welfare or cause or "issue" organizations. They have no limits on lobbying, and political campaign activity must not be the primary endeavor. They too are subject to IRC Section 4958 on "excess benefit" penalties and, more recently, to the vague "commerciality" doctrine.

- ◆ IRC Section 501(c)(6). Technically called "business leagues," these are trade associations, professional societies, and chambers of commerce. They have no limits on lobbying nor political campaign activity if the latter is not the primary endeavor. Political campaign contributions from organization funds are prohibited for these and all corporations at the federal level; they are subject to a tax if made at the state or local levels when permitted of corporations. Dues paid to these organizations are declared by IRC Section 162(e)(3) to be nondeductible for members to the extent of the organizations' lobbying and political activities.

- All of the organizations in these categories of federal income tax exemption (with exceptions not pertinent here) are subject to IRC Section 512 on unrelated business income tax ("UBIT"); they pay income tax on the net return of activities not substantially related to their exempt purposes. For UBIT to be applicable, there must be: (1) a "business" activity, that is (2) "regularly carried on" and that (3) "is not substantially related" to the organization's exempt purposes (i.e., does not "contribute importantly" to those exempt purposes per the U.S. Supreme Court's interpretation in *American College of Physicians*). The net financial gain (i.e., revenues less expenses) from all of an organization's UBIT-eligible activities (e.g., where gains exceed losses) is subject to regular federal corporate income tax. UBIT generally does not apply to rent, royalties, interest, dividends, or capital gains (with an exception for debt-financed assets).

- The most common kinds of activities that generate UBIT-eligible revenue include: advertising, insurance, fee-based individual consulting/testing, and so on. Trade show/exhibition revenue has statutory protection from treatment as UBIT-eligible under most circumstances per IRC Section 513(d)(3)(B).

- Where an exempt organization realizes "substantial" UBIT-eligible revenue, the organization will no longer qualify for federal income tax exemption at all. There is no clear level or percentage of what constitutes "substantial." If an exempt organization begins to realize UBIT-eligible revenue that could be considered "substantial" and therefore threatening to the organization's exempt status, the conventional way to manage the risk is to create a for-profit subsidiary.

- Substantial *gross or net revenue* generated from the unrelated activity is the most obvious danger signal that should trigger consideration of a for-profit subsidiary. But there are some other fact patterns in which a for-profit subsidiary may be desirable:

- A high percentage of *staff time* devoted to an unrelated business activity is also a danger signal. The Internal Revenue Service (IRS) routinely looks to the percentage of the time devoted to the unrelated business activity by paid employees to determine whether the activity is substantial. This percentage can be readily ascertainable, because the organization usually allocates a percentage of its salaries to its unrelated activity as an offset to income from the unrelated activity. The IRS thus needs only to compare the deduction on an organization's Form 990-T, the tax return for unrelated business income activities, to the total salaries shown on Form 990, the information return for tax-exempt activities, to determine what percentage of staff time is allocable to the unrelated activity. An organization might make the mistake of allocating a high percentage of staff time to unrelated activities to generate substantial expenses that will offset income from the unrelated activities. It is thus creating what amounts to an admission that the unrelated activities are substantial in relation to the organization's exempt activities.

- Generation of *loss* by the unrelated activity is a third danger signal. If the unrelated activity is consistently generating a substantial loss, this may indicate to the IRS that the excess of expenses over income may be offsetting otherwise taxable income from other unrelated activities of the organization or being covered by the related, exempt income of the organization. If the loss is substantial, the IRS could consider this an abuse of tax-exempt status. It may be advisable to create a for-profit subsidiary to avoid this situation.

- In addition to protecting an exempt organization's federal income tax exempt status, there are often other reasons to create an owned and controlled for-profit taxable subsidiary. These reasons could enhance the rationale for proceeding when tax considerations result in a close call. They include: (1) encouraging entrepreneurship in particular business-type endeavors; (2) separating from the "parent" organization activity that has special legal liability exposure; or (3) developing a streamlined or different governance structure from that of the parent.

- Associations and other exempt organizations often conduct activities that are related only in part, and unrelated in part, to their exempt purposes. In such cases, only the income generated by the unrelated activity is subject to tax, and the organization may deduct only those expenses specifically allocable to the unrelated portion of the business activity. It is common to have net revenue from the unrelated portion of the activity but to have net loss when the activity is considered as a whole. In such cases, it may be advisable to create a for-profit subsidiary so that the entire income from the activity, and all of the expenses attributable to it, will be counted in determining income.

- It is not likely that the IRS would require separate boards of directors or separate headquarters for exempt organizations and for their for-profit taxable subsidiaries. Some differentiation from the roster of the "parent" organization's governing board and that of the subsidiary may be warranted to enhance the defensibility of the entities as two separate ones. The IRS does clearly require strict financial separation. There must be a very precise allocation of all of the expenses of the main organization and the subsidiary that are in any way related. Furthermore, it is important to be able to substantiate the allocation on audit. For example, staff time should be allocated by having employees keep an accurate daily log of the number of hours devoted to the matters of the for-profit subsidiary. Legal and accounting fees should be allocated by the service provider. A separate log may be kept for equipment, telephone, and mail expenses.

- Another way to achieve the necessary financial separation is to have the for-profit subsidiary retain the main organization to manage it and to pay a management fee. Care must be taken to have the management fee approximate the fair market value of the services. It may be advisable to ask for quotes from association management companies or others for the same services. These quotes can be shown to the IRS as substantiation for the fair market value of the service fee paid by the subsidiary to the main organization. Note that the management fee, less expenses, may in some circumstances be considered unrelated business income to the main organization.

- It is desirable to have a written agreement between the main organization and its for-profit subsidiary that sets out an "arm's length" arrangement for purchase of services by the subsidiary from the main organization. This agreement—often called a "cost-sharing agreement" or "service contract"—also can serve as an internal policy guide to help ensure complete financial separation is maintained between the two entities.

- Separate from considerations of tax exemption, another major reason for conducting a new program through a subsidiary, rather than through the main organization, is the desire to isolate the organization from liability for the program if possible.

- As associations and other exempt organizations become more innovative, more aggressive, and more visible in their policies or activities, they inevitably also become "lightning rods" for legal claims. In the 1982 *Hydrolevel* case, the Supreme Court held an engineering society responsible for the first time for antitrust treble damages because of an anticompetitive interpretation of product standards that the lower level staff and volunteers of the society had issued. In doing so, the Court declared that in some circumstances a private organization can become virtually "an extra-governmental agency, which prescribes rules for the regulation of interstate commerce," and that associations are "rife with opportunities" to violate the antitrust laws.

- Apart from antitrust, associations and other exempt organizations increasingly are named as defendants in personal injury or property damage cases because of communications, standards, or policies issued by the organizations that are claimed to have caused injury or damage.

- As associations and other exempt organizations expand into new services for members or other constituents that sometimes more closely resemble those offered by commercial enterprises, they are becoming entangled in the myriad disputes that seems symptomatic of American business operations—claims for contract violation, copyright or trademark infringement, and the like.

- One strategy that may help to protect the assets and reputation of an organization against antitrust, tort damage, and other kinds of claims for liability from a new service is to offer the service through an independently incorporated subsidiary.

- The extent to which an organization can successfully isolate itself from liability arising through a separate subsidiary corporation will always depend on the specific situation of the organization and its subsidiary. Predictions on this subject are unreliable because there is as yet almost no precedent on liability of a nonprofit parent for the claimed misdeeds of its subsidiary. Generally, however, one can look for guidance to the body of law that has grown up on the subject of commercial corporation liability for the illegal or harmful acts or omissions of its incorporated subsidiaries. Here one finds that courts typically focus on two fundamental elements:

  - The extent of control exercised by the parent over the subsidiary.

  - The extent to which the parent actually participated in the challenged policy or activity.

- The cases on corporate parent liability for incorporated subsidiaries discuss the extent of control a parent can exercise over its subsidiary before the subsidiary loses its separate legal existence and must be considered a "mere instrumentality" of the parent. In these cases, courts will "pierce the corporate veil" of the subsidiary and hold the parent liable.

- Likewise, if it can be shown that the parent participated in the claimed wrongdoing of the subsidiary, the "mere instrumentality" rule is unnecessary. The parent will be held responsible for its own participation and the consequences of the wrongdoing.

- Associations and other exempt organizations may have as one purpose the isolation of themselves from potential liability for new services when they consider offering the new services through separately incorporated subsidiaries. If that is a purpose, it is important to plan for the issues of control and participation to maximize the likelihood of legal isolation between the main organization and the subsidiary.

- Although it should certainly not deter an association or other exempt organization from proceeding to form an owned and controlled subsidiary where other factors argue for proceeding with one, it should be born in mind that the circumstances and finances of the arrangement will likely be subject to public disclosure.

- The kinds of exempt organizations addressed here are required to file annual informational tax reports/returns with the IRS. The Form 990 is an informational report; where there is UBIT-eligible income, the Form 990-T is filed also for other purposes, such as when the proxy tax is paid in lieu of dues nondeductibility disclosure because of lobbying expenditures. The Form 990 is a public document [as is the Form 990-T for Section 501 (c)(3) organizations]. IRS will release these filings to members of the public upon request. Some public interest Web sites obtain these forms and publish them. An exempt organization is required to share copies of the last three years' Forms 990, plus the IRS tax-exemption determination and any correspondence regarding the determination that is available, to any member of the public who requests them from the organization per IRC Section 6104.

- The Form 990 annual informational return, revised in 2007–8 and required for use starting in 2009, requires disclosure of information about subsidiaries.

- Associations and other exempt organizations are expanding the nature and scope of their endeavors. Neither tax exemption nor legal liability restrains the offering of creative and innovative services to members. For many, subsidiaries provide the appropriate legal vehicle to use in providing new services.

Chapter 81 Resources

Books

ABA Committee on Nonprofit Corporations. *Guide for Directors of Nonprofit Corporations, Section Edition*. Chicago: American Bar Association Section of Business Law, 2002, p. 91.

Cipriani. "Establishing an Affiliated Organization." In *Associations and the Law*. Jacobs, ed. Washington, D.C.: American Society of Association Executives, 2002, p. 114.

Hart. "How to Use Subsidiaries: Use of For-Profit Subsidiaries Outside the Joint Venture Context." In *1999 Legal Symposium*. Washington, D.C.: American Society of Association Executives, 1999.

Hopkins. *The Law of Tax-Exempt Organizations, 8th ed*. Hoboken, N.J.: John Wiley, 2003, p. 918; 2006 Cum. Supp. 157.

Tenenbaum. *Association Tax Compliance Guide*. Washington, D.C.: American Society of Association Executives, 2000. p. 58.

Sanders. "Tax Planning for Joint Ventures: How to Use For-Profit Subsidiaries." In *1999 Legal Symposium*. Washington, D.C.: American Society of Association Executives, 1999.

Articles

Chiechi. "Exempt Parent Can Have For-Profit Subsidiary." *Journal of Taxation* (November 1987): 362.

Cases

United States v. American College of Physicians, 475 U.S. 834 (1986). Supreme Court determination that advertising in a professional medical journal is primarily for the production of revenue and thus unrelated to the exempt purposes of the organization that publishes the journal because the advertising did not "contribute importantly" to those exempt purposes.

American Soc'y of Mechanical Eng'rs, Inc. v. Hydrolevel Corp., 456 U.S. 556 (1982). Ground-breaking Supreme Court ruling in which an association was found vicariously responsible for antitrust violations committed by low-level staff and volunteers with no knowledge by, approval from, or benefit for the association's governing board.

Jack Russell Terrier Network v. Am. Kennel Club, Inc., 407 F.3d 1027 (9th Cir. 2005). National association and its local chartered chapter found not to be subject to an antitrust conspiracy accusation based on the relatedness of the two organizations; may also apply in situations of parent/subsidiary.

Chapter 87
IRS Forms & Procedures

The Internal Revenue Service (IRS) has promulgated detailed forms and procedures for associations and other organizations to use in seeking determinations of federal income tax-exempt status, appealing adverse determinations on exempt status, filing annual informational returns, and filing annual tax returns for any unrelated business income. As of 2009, the Form 990 annual informational tax return required of most tax-exempt organizations was dramatically revised and expanded to include not only very extensive financial disclosure but also very extensive disclosure of legal and governance issues. This chapter summarizes the applicable IRS forms and procedures.

Summary

- There are initial and continuing procedural requirements promulgated by the IRS for associations and other nonprofit organizations to follow in seeking to obtain determinations of federal income tax-exempt status and maintaining that status.

- For those seeking determinations of tax-exempt status as business leagues under Section 501(c)(6) of the Internal Revenue Code (IRC), which will include most trade associations and professional societies, IRS Form 1024 is to be used.

- For those seeking determinations of exempt status as charitable, educational, scientific, religious, amateur sports, or other similar types of organizations listed under Section 501(c)(3) of the Code, IRS Form 1023 is to be used.

- A request for written determination of exempt status must be made within 27 months (Form 1023) or 15 months (Form 1024) after the end of the month in which the organization was created in order for an eventual determination to be retroactive to the date of creation. If an organization does not file within the specified period, exemption will be effective as of the date of its application for exempt status. There are various exceptions and special rules in the IRS guidelines.

- If an organization receives an adverse determination of exempt status, it may file a protest and seek a conference with the Regional Appeals Office having jurisdiction over the Key District Office that issued the adverse determination. The protest must be filed within 30 days from the date of the determination letter and must be filed with the Key District Office. The organization may obtain review by the IRS at the National Office level either on request by the organization or the Key District Office by means of a Technical Advice procedure. Once the administrative levels of review are exhausted by the organization, it may sue the IRS in a federal district court in the form of a tax refund suit alleging that the adverse determination was incorrect. It may refuse to pay any tax assessed and file a petition in the U.S. Tax Court claiming tax-exempt status. In the case of an organization seeking exempt status under Section 501(c)(3), it may sue for a declaratory judgment in the U.S. Tax Court.

- Revocation of federal income tax exempt status from an organization is processed by the IRS under procedures similar to those used upon the issuance of an adverse determination of exempt status. Revocation is generally announced by the Key District Office. Appeals may be available at the Regional Appeals Office and National Office under certain circumstances. The same judicial remedies described above also are applicable.

- Organizations determined to be exempt from taxation under either Section 501(c)(6) or Section 501(c)(3), as well as other categories, are required to file annual informational returns unless they do not normally have gross receipts of more than $25,000 in each taxable year. Thus the Form 990 requirement applies to most trade associations, professional societies, social welfare organizations, and charities (other than churches and schools). And most organizations are now required to file their Forms 990 electronically. Legislation enacted in 2006 requires Section 501(c)(3) tax-exempt entities with less than $25,000 in gross annual receipts, which were previously exempt from filing, to file electronic informational notices (referred to as the "e-Postcard" or Form 990-N) with various information, including evidence that the organization continues to qualify for its tax exemption. While there is no monetary penalty associated with failure to observe this provision, the IRS will revoke an entity's tax exemption if it fails to file a notice for three consecutive years. Forms 990 will be made available by the IRS for public inspection. In addition, some public-interest organizations obtain many Forms 990 from the IRS or from the filing organizations and post them on their Web sites. Finally, as noted below, the organizations themselves have an obligation to disclose to members of the public when requested their Forms 990, as well as other tax exemption information, under certain parameters.

- After extensive and much-publicized inquiries and investigations by the U.S. Congress, the IRS substantially revised and expanded the Form 990 informational return during the 2007–8 period. The new form is required to be used by Form 990 filers for tax years beginning on or after January 1, 2008. Unless an organization seeks and obtains an extension, Form 990 is due by the 15th day of the fifth month following the close of the organization's fiscal/tax year. So the newest version, Form 990 (2008), was to be first used beginning May 15, 2009. The IRS had not updated Form 990 since 1979 and was prompted to do so in part as a result of reports of abuse of tax-exempt status by some organizations. The stated goals of the form revision effort are to enhance transparency for the government and the public, to promote tax compliance by accurately reflecting an exempt organization's activities, and to minimize organizations' filing burdens.

• Form 990 (2008) includes a core form and supplemental schedules regarding specific organizational activities and financial information. It requires increased reporting in areas such as governance, compensation, tax-exempt bonds, foreign activities, and non-cash contributions.

• For each schedule, the instructions provide an overview of its purpose, an explanation of who is required to file it, and line-by-line instructions. The Form 990 (2008) instructions include a glossary of key terms used in the form, a sequencing list to assist organizations in deciding the order in which to complete parts and schedules of the form (found in the general instructions), and a compensation table to help organizations determine what items of compensation and benefits to report and where.

• In total, the core form, instructions, and related documents for Form 990 (2008) number over 300 pages of text; for associations or other tax-exempt organizations to familiarize themselves with the requirements is a substantial undertaking that should be planned will in advance of not only the organization's filing date but also in advance of the end of the applicable tax year.

• Among the major legal and governance features of Form 990 (2008), separate from the many financial disclosures required, are these:

   ◆ Part IV, 12. Whether there are audited financial statements prepared per GAAP.

   ◆ Part IV, 14A. Disclosure of any office, employees, or agents outside the United States.

   ◆ Part IV, 14B. Whether there were aggregate revenues or expenses of more than $10,000 from grant making, fund-raising, business, or program service activities outside the United States.

♦ Part IV, 17-19. Whether there was more than $15,000 in fund-raising expenses.

♦ Part IV, 28. Whether any person who is a current or former officer, director, trustee, or "key employee" (for which IRS provides an elaborate definition): (a) has a business relationship, (b) has a family member with a business relationship, or (c) serves with an entity doing business with the organization.

♦ Part VI, 1a. The number of voting members of the governing board.

♦ Part VI, 1b. The number of voting members of the governing board who are "independent" (which is defined).

♦ Part VI, 8a. Whether there is contemporaneous documentation (i.e., minutes) of meetings held, or written actions undertaken, by the governing board.

♦ Part VI, 8b. Whether there are minutes of meetings of each committee with authority to act on behalf of the governing board.

♦ Part VI, 9a. Whether there are local chapters, branches, or affiliates.

♦ Part VI, 9b. If so, what written policies and procedures govern the activities of those chapters, affiliates, and branches to ensure their operations are consistent with those of the main organization.

♦ Part VI, 10. Whether a copy of the Form 990 was provided to the organization's governing body before it was filed (all organizations must describe in Schedule O, the process, if any, the organization uses to review the Form 990).

♦ Part VI, 19. A description in Schedule O whether (and if so, how) the organization makes its governing documents, conflict of interest policy, and financial statements available to the public.

♦ Part IX, 11. What fees for services (of non-employees) are paid for lobbying.

♦ Part IX, 18. Whether there are payments of travel or entertainment expenses for any federal, state, or local public officials.

♦ Part XI, 2b. Whether the organization's financial statements were audited by an independent accountant.

♦ Part XI, 2c. If yes, whether the organization has a committee that assumes responsibility for oversight of the audit, review, or compilation of its financial statements and selection of an independent accountant.

- In addition, Form 990 (2008) asks whether the filing organization has five separate policies/procedures that the IRS believes are important for good governance. It is not made clear what are the consequences of an organization stating on its Form 990 that it did not have one or more of these policies/procedures in place during the fiscal/tax year for which the Form 990 is being filed. But negative answers could presumably attract the attention of the IRS. And, at any rate, the IRS expects that compliance will be compelled by exempt organizations wishing to avoid any possible embarrassment or criticism by their members or donors, the press, or others who observe and form impressions of the organizations' diligence in maintaining appropriate legal and governance policies and procedures. The singular policies/procedures flagged on Form 990 are these:

  - Conflict of Interest Policy. This policy is intended by the IRS to: (1) define conflicts of interest; (2) identify classes of individuals within the organization covered by the policy; (3) facilitate disclosure of information that may help identify conflicts of interest; and (4) specify procedures to be followed in managing conflicts of interest.

  - Whistleblower Policy. This policy is intended to: (1) encourage staff and volunteers to come forward with credible information on illegal practices or serious violations of adopted policies of the organization; (2) specify that the organization will protect the person from retaliation; and (3) identify where such information can be reported.

  - Document Retention and Destruction Policy. This policy, for which the IRS gives little direction, is intended to identify the record retention responsibilities of staff, volunteers, members of the governing board, and outsiders for maintaining and documenting the storage and destruction of the organization's documents and records.

  - Procedure for Determining Compensation for the Chief Employed Executive, and Other Officers or "Key Employees." Here, Form 990 (2008) asks separately if a specified procedure is following by the organization in determining the compensation, on one hand, of the chief employed executive, or, on the other hand, of other officers or "key employees" of the organization. In each case the procedure that the IRS specifies would include all of these elements: (1) review and approval by unbiased members of the organization's governing board or its compensation committee; (2) use of reasonable data as to comparable compensation; and (3) contemporaneous documentation and recordkeeping of who made the decisions and what comparability data were used.

♦ (Contingent) Joint Venture Policy. Here, the organization is asked whether it has joint ventures or other similar arrangements with taxable business entities. "Other similar arrangements" are not defined by the IRS but presumably would be limited to arrangements in which the tax-exempt organization and a taxable business entity share ownership, profits and losses, and governance of a venture, whether the venture is structured via a contract, partnership, limited liability company ("LLC") or otherwise. "Other similar arrangements" would not include conventional sponsorships/endorsements by an exempt organization of a commercial vendor's products or services in return for mere receipt of royalty revenue by the organization. Under Form 990, if the filing organization indicates that it does have joint ventures or other similar arrangements with taxable business entities, the organization is then asked whether it has a policy in place to evaluate its participation in joint venture arrangements under federal tax law and take steps to safeguard the organization's exempt status with respect to such arrangements.

• An organization that is seeking a tax-exempt status determination from the IRS, but has not yet received it, may nevertheless file its informational return as an exempt organization but should indicate on the form that its request is pending. This procedure will release the organization from possible penalties and interest and will likewise commence the applicable statute of limitations.

• Exempt organizations that have unrelated business income over $1,000 in a taxable year must report that income on IRS Form 990-T. Regular corporate income taxes apply to net taxable income reported on Form 990-T.

• An exempt organization that has undergone a dissolution, termination, or other major disposition of assets must file a final informational return on IRS Form 990, 990-EZ, or e-Postcard (990-N) as appropriate. The IRS has announced that the return/report is due four months and 15 days following the triggering event.

• Organizations that fail to file required returns or reports to the IRS may be subject to penalties of $20 per day of delinquency. The maximum penalty is the lesser of $10,000 or 5 percent of gross receipts for the year. For exempt organizations with $1,000,000 or more in gross receipts, the penalty for failure to file timely, or to include correct information, is $100 per day of delinquency, up to $50,000 maximum. No penalty is imposed if reasonable cause can be shown.

• In 1987, Congress required that (1) non-Section 501(c)(3) tax-exempt organizations disclose to contributors that their contributions are not tax deductible as charitable contributions, and (2) tax-exempt organizations permit public inspection of their annual tax returns to the IRS and applications for exempt status.

- Non-Section 501(c)(3) tax-exempt organizations [including those exempt under Section 501(c)(6)] that have more than $100,000 in annual gross receipts, a well as political organizations, are required to disclose in their fund-raising solicitations that contributions or gifts to them are not charitable contributions for federal income tax deduction purposes. The IRS has provided several alternative disclosure statements to use. One is: "Contributions or gifts to [name of organization] are not tax deductible as charitable contributions." Another is for use if the solicitation is for dues that are normally deductible as business expenses: "Contributions or gifts to [name of organization] are not tax deductible as charitable contributions. However, they may be tax deductible as ordinary and necessary business expenses." The statement must be (1) in print at least the size of the soliciting message, (2) in the first sentence of a paragraph or its own paragraph, and (3) included on the message side of any material to be returned with the contribution. Other directives exist for telephone, television, and radio solicitations.

- Exempt organizations also are required to make their annual information returns available for public inspection during normal business hours at the organizations' principal offices and, in some cases, at regional or district offices as well. The required disclosure of the annual return includes exact copies of the original Forms 990 for a three-year period and all schedules and attachments filed with the IRS, excluding the names and addresses of the organization's contributors. However, the disclosure requirement does not apply to Form 990-T for unrelated business income [except for Section 501(c)(3) organizations] or Form 120-POL for political committees. Exemption application materials that must be made public include the application itself; supporting documents, such as responses to IRS questions; and IRS letters or documents regarding the application. A requester must be permitted to take notes or copy the documents on the requester's own copying equipment (which, of course, would require removal of the documents); alternatively, if the requester does not object, the documents may be copied by the association and the requester charged $1 for the first page and $0.15 for subsequent pages.

- Organizations exempt under Section 501(c)(3), uniquely, are also required to make public disclosure of their Forms 990-T for unrelated business income tax; this requirement is effective only for Forms 990-T filed after the August 2006 enactment of the requirement.

- The correct use of IRS forms and procedures for tax-exempt organizations can result in important advantages just as incorrect use can defeat, delay, or jeopardize the organizations' aims. The laws affecting tax-exempt organizations are often strikingly different from those affecting business corporations. Tax-exempt organization legal and accounting practice is a specialty not maintained by most lawyers or accountants. Exempt organizations should seek out specialists in exempt organization law when assistance is needed.

Chapter 87 Resources

Books
Hopkins. *The Law of Tax-Exempt Organizations, 8th ed.* Hoboken, N.J.: John Wiley, 2003, p. 653; 2006 Cum. Supp. 111.
Tenenbaum. *Association Tax Compliance Guide.* Washington, D.C.: American Society of Association Executives, 2000. p. 95.

Articles
Elias. "New Disclosure Regulations for Tax-Exempt Organizations." *Association Law & Policy* (April 1, 1999): 3.
Hodges. "Practical Considerations in Establishing a Section 501(c)(3) Organization." *Taxation of Exempts* (Sept./Oct. 2002): 51

Regulations
Regulations Sections 601.201 (N)(5) and (6).

New Sample Documents

14A
Basic Form 990 Governance Policies/Procedures

Note: The Internal Revenue Service in 2007-08 issued a revised Form 990 annual informational tax return/report [referred to as Form 990 (2008)] that must be submitted by most federal income tax exempt organizations, including trade associations, professional societies, cause/social welfare groups, and charitable/scientific/educational organizations. Instructions for the form were also issued during that period. The revised Form 990 is the IRS's reaction to concerns expressed by key committees in Congress for greater disclosure and improved governance in nonprofit tax-exempt organizations. The IRS also asserts its view that appropriate governance enhances compliance with federal income tax exemption requirements. Among other features, the form asks in Part VI if the filing organization has adopted a series of five governance policies or procedures; the organization must answer "yes" or "no" for each. Although a "no" answer does not indicate any violation of law or inconsistency with federal income tax exemption requirements, it could trigger scrutiny by the IRS. It could also reflect adversely on an organization in the eyes of its members, donors, or others. Most organizations will want to be able to answer "yes" to all five of these governance questions. The method of adoption is not specified by the IRS, but it would be typical for such policies or procedures to be adopted by the organization's principal governing body, such as its board of directors, or by a committee delegated to do so by the board. Presented here are sample governance policies or procedures for non-profit tax-exempt organizations in basic versions that reflect the narrowly defined IRS definitions/instructions for Part VI of Form 990 (2008). Each would likely be sufficient to permit the organization to respond "yes" to the Form 990 question about that policy. Many organizations may prefer expanded or enhanced versions of the policies; if the essential elements are maintained, those should still suffice for Form 990 purposes. More elaborate versions for some, such as conflicts of interest or document retention/destruction, are provided elsewhere in this Documents Supplement. Note that one of these policies/procedures, that on joint ventures, is contingent; the IRS only asks if the filing organization has the policy if the organization indicates that it maintains joint ventures as the IRS describes them.

Policies and Procedures

A. Conflict of Interest Policy

This <u>Conflict of Interest Policy</u> of [insert the name of the "Organization"]: (1) defines conflicts of interest; (2) identifies classes of individuals within the Organization covered by this policy; (3) facilitates disclosure of information that may help identify conflicts of interest; and (4) specifies procedures to be followed in managing conflicts of interest.

    1. **Definition of conflicts of interest**. A conflict of interest arises when a person in a position of authority over the Organization may benefit financially from a decision he or she could make in that capacity, including indirect benefits such as to family members or businesses with which the person is closely associated. This policy is focused upon material financial interest of, or benefit to, such persons.

    2. **Individuals covered**. Persons covered by this policy are the Organization's officers, directors, chief employed executive, and chief employed finance executive.

    3. **Facilitation of disclosure**. Persons covered by this policy will annually disclose or update to the Chairman of the Board of Directors on a form provided by the Organization their interests that could give rise to conflicts of interest, such as a list of family members, substantial business or investment holdings, and other transactions or affiliations with businesses and other organizations or those of family members.

    4. **Procedures to manage conflicts**. For each interest disclosed to the Chairman of the Board of Directors, the Chairman will determine whether to: (a) take no action; (b) assure full disclosure to the Board of Directors and other individuals covered by this policy; (c) ask the person to recuse from participation in related discussions or decisions within the Organization; or (d) ask the person to resign from his or her position in the Organization or, if the person refuses to resign, become subject to possible removal in accordance with the Organization's removal procedures. The Organization's chief employed executive and chief employed finance executive will monitor proposed or ongoing transactions for conflicts of interest and disclose them to the Chairman of the Board of Directors in order to deal with potential or actual conflicts, whether discovered before or after the transaction has occurred.

B. Whistleblower Protection Policy

This <u>Whistleblower Protection Policy</u> of [insert the name of the "Organization"]: (1) encourages staff and volunteers to come forward with credible information on illegal practices or serious violations of adopted policies of the Organization; (2) specifies that the Organization will protect the person from retaliation; and (3) identifies where such information can be reported.

    1. **Encouragement of reporting**. The Organization encourages complaints, reports, or inquiries about illegal practices or serious violations of the Organization's policies, including illegal or improper conduct by the

Organization itself, by its leadership, or by others on its behalf. Appropriate subjects to raise under this policy would include financial improprieties, accounting or audit matters, ethical violations, or other similar illegal or improper practices or policies. Other subjects on which the Organization has existing complaint mechanisms should be addressed under those mechanisms, such as raising matters of alleged discrimination or harassment via the Organization's human resources channels, unless those channels are themselves implicated in the wrongdoing. This policy is not intended to provide a means of appeal from outcomes in those other mechanisms.

2. **Protection from retaliation**. The Organization prohibits retaliation by or on behalf of the Organization against staff or volunteers for making good faith complaints, reports, or inquiries under this policy or for participating in a review or investigation under this policy. This protection extends to those whose allegations are made in good faith but prove to be mistaken. The Organization reserves the right to discipline persons, including termination of their employment, if they make bad faith, knowingly false, or vexatious complaints, reports or inquiries, or otherwise abuse this policy.

3. **Where to report**. Complaints, reports, or inquiries may be made under this policy on a confidential or anonymous basis. They should describe in detail the specific facts demonstrating the bases for the complaints, reports, or inquiries. They should be directed to the Organization's chief employed executive or Chairman of the Board of Directors; if both of those persons are implicated in the complaint, report, or inquiry, it should be directed to [insert title of individual]. The Organization will conduct a prompt, discreet, and objective review or investigation. Staff or volunteers must recognize that the Organization may be unable to fully evaluate a vague or general complaint, report, or inquiry that is made anonymously, or report the result to the initiating volunteer or staff.

C. Document Retention and Destruction Policy

This <u>Document Retention and Destruction Policy</u> of [insert the name of the "Organization"] identifies the record retention responsibilities of staff, volunteers, members of the Board of Directors, and outsiders for maintaining and documenting the storage and destruction of the Organization's documents and records.

1. **Rules**. The Organization's staff, volunteers, members of the Board of Directors, and outsiders (i.e., independent contractors via agreements with them) are required to honor these rules: (a) paper or electronic documents indicated under the terms for retention below will be transferred and maintained by the Human Resources, Legal, or Administrative staffs/departments or their equivalents; (b) all other paper documents will be destroyed after three years; (c) all other electronic documents will be deleted from all individual computers, databases, networks, and backup

storage after one year; and (d) no paper or electronic documents will be destroyed or deleted if pertinent to any ongoing or anticipated government investigation or proceeding or private litigation.

   2. **Terms for retention**.

   a. Retain <u>permanently</u>:

>   *Governance records*—Charter and amendments, bylaws, other organizational documents, governing board and board committee minutes.
>   *Tax records*—Filed state and federal tax returns/reports and supporting records, tax exemption determination letter and related correspondence, files related to tax audits.
>   *Intellectual property records*—Copyright and trademark registrations and samples of protected works.
>   *Financial records*—Audited financial statements, attorney contingent liability letters.

   b. Retain <u>for ten years</u>:

>   *Pension and benefit records*—Pension (ERISA) plan participant/beneficiary records, actuarial reports, related correspondence with government agencies, and supporting records.
>   *Government relations records*—State and federal lobbying and political contribution reports and supporting records.

   c. Retain <u>for three years</u>:

>   *Employee/employment records*—Employee names, addresses, social security numbers, dates of birth, INS Form I-9s, résumé/application materials, job descriptions, dates of hire and termination/separation, evaluations, compensation information, promotions, transfers, disciplinary matters, time/payroll records, leave/comp time/FMLA, engagement and discharge correspondence, documentation of basis for independent contractor status (retain for all current employees and independent contractors and for three years after departure of each individual).
>   *Lease, insurance, and contract/license records*—Software license agreements; vendor, hotel, and service agreements; independent contractor agreements; employment agreements; consultant agreements; and all other agreements (retain during the term of the agreement and for three years after the termination, expiration or nonrenewal of each agreement).

   d. Retain <u>for one year</u>:

>   *All other electronic records, documents, and files*—Correspondence files, past budgets, bank statements, publications, employee manuals/policies and procedures, survey information.

   3. **Exceptions**. Exceptions to these rules and terms for retention may be granted only by the Organization's chief staff executive or Chairman of the Board.

D. Procedure for Determining Compensation

This Procedure for Determining Compensation of [insert the name of the "Organization"] applies to the compensation of the following persons employed by the Organization:

_____ The Organization's **chief employed executive**[1]

[CHECK IF APPLICABLE]

_____ Other **Officers**[2] or **Key Employees**[3] of the Organization by title:_____

_____ [CHECK IF APPLICABLE; SUPPLY TITLES].

The procedure includes all of these elements: (1) review and approval by the Board of Directors or Compensation Committee of the Organization; (2) use of data as to comparable compensation; and (3) contemporaneous documentation and recordkeeping.

1. **Review and approval**. The compensation of the person is reviewed and approved by the Board of Directors or Compensation Committee of the Organization, provided that persons with conflicts of interest with respect to the compensation arrangement at issue are not involved in this review and approval.

2. **Use of data as to comparable compensation**. The compensation of the person is reviewed and approved using data as to comparable compensation for similarly qualified persons in functionally comparable positions at similarly situated organizations.

3. **Contemporaneous documentation and recordkeeping**. There is contemporaneous documentation and recordkeeping with respect to the deliberations and decisions regarding the compensation arrangement.

---

[1] **Chief employed executive**—The CEO (i.e., Chief Executive Officer), executive director, or top management official (i.e., a person who has ultimate responsibility for implementing the decisions of the Organization's governing body or for supervising the management, administration, or operations of the Organization).

[2] **Officer**—A person elected or appointed to manage the Organization's daily operations, such as a president, vice president, secretary, or treasurer. The officers of the Organization are determined by reference to its organizing document, bylaws, or resolutions of its governing body, or as otherwise designated consistent with state law, but at a minimum include those officers required by applicable state law. Include as officers the Organization's top management official and top financial official (the person who has ultimate responsibility for managing the Organization's finances).

[3] **Key Employee**—An employee of the Organization who meets all three of the following tests: (1) $150,000 Test: receives reportable compensation from the Organization and all related organizations in excess of $150,000 for the year; (2) Responsibility Test: the employee: (a) has responsibility, powers, or influence over the Organization as a whole that is similar to those of officers, directors, or trustees; (b) manages a discrete segment or activity of the Organization that represents 10% or more of the activities, assets, income, or expenses of the Organization, as compared to the Organization as a whole; or (c) has or shares authority to control or determine 10% or more of the Organization's capital expenditures, operating budget, or compensation for employees; and (3) Top 20 Test: is one of the 20 employees (that satisfy the $150,000 Test and Responsibility Test) with the highest reportable compensation from the Organization and related organizations for the year.

E. Contingent Joint Venture Policy

This <u>Joint Venture Policy</u> of [insert the name of the "Organization"] requires that the Organization evaluate its participation in joint venture arrangements under Federal tax law and take steps to safeguard the Organization's exempt status with respect to such arrangements. It applies to any joint ownership or contractual arrangement through which there is an agreement to jointly undertake a specific business enterprise, investment, or exempt-purpose activity as further defined in this policy.

    1. **Joint ventures or similar arrangements with taxable entities**. For purposes of this policy, a joint venture or similar arrangement (or a "venture or arrangement") means any joint ownership or contractual arrangement through which there is an agreement to jointly undertake a specific business enterprise, investment, or exempt-purpose activity without regard to: (a) whether the Organization controls the venture or arrangement; (b) the legal structure of the venture or arrangement; or (c) whether the venture or arrangement is taxed as a partnership or as an association or corporation for federal income tax purposes. A venture or arrangement is disregarded if it meets both of the following conditions:

> (i) 95% or more of the venture's or arrangement's income for its tax year ending within the Organization's tax year is excluded from unrelated business income taxation [including but not limited to: *(a)* dividends, interest, and annuities; *(b)* royalties; *(c)* rent from real property and incidental related personal property except to the extent of debt-financing; and *(d)* gains or losses from the sale of property]; and
>
> (ii) the primary purpose of the Organization's contribution to, or investment or participation in, the venture or arrangement is the production of income or appreciation of property.

    2. **Safeguards to ensure exempt status protection**. The Organization will: (a) negotiate in its transactions and arrangements with other members of the venture or arrangement such terms and safeguards adequate to ensure that the Organization's exempt status is protected; and (b) take steps to safeguard the Organization's exempt status with respect to the venture or arrangement. Some examples of safeguards include:

> (i) control over the venture or arrangement sufficient to ensure that it furthers the exempt purpose of the organization;
>
> (ii) requirements that the venture or arrangement gives priority to exempt purposes over maximizing profits for the other participants;
>
> (iii) requirements that the venture or arrangement not engage in activities that would jeopardize the Organization's exemption; and
>
> (iv) requirements that all contracts entered into with the organization be on terms that are arm's length or more favorable to the Organization.

14B
Compliance Policy on Semi-Annual Certification Regarding Gifts/Travel

Note: The federal lobbying laws not only regulate registration and reporting but also gifts, travel, and honoraria provided to Members and employees of the U.S. Congress. Since 2007 the burden of compliance falls not only upon federal officials but also upon lobbyists, foreign agents, and their employers, including associations. Criminal and strict civil penalties apply to violations and are enforced by the U.S. Department of Justice. This "Compliance Policy on Semi-Annual Certification Regarding Gifts/Travel" is intended to assist associations and other nonprofit organizations in managing the risks that arise because of the broad sweep of the law. In addition to quarterly reports of lobbying activities and expenditures, the law requires semi-annual certification of compliance with its gifts, travel, and honoraria provisions. This policy includes a series of documents that may help those already engaged in federal lobbying to ensure that all employees are aware of the "dos and don'ts" on gifts/travel. The policy includes: (1) a <u>Model Employee Letter</u> to be sent to all employees along with a Fact Sheet to remind them of the organization's obligations under the federal lobbying law provisions; (2) a <u>Model Policy</u> providing suggested language to be used for internal policies on compliance; and (3) a <u>Model Internal "Attestation Letter"</u> that can be elicited from department or branch heads or other staff leadership to help the person who must certify compliance for the organization be assured that there is proper basis for the certification. This set of documents should be modified to fit the individual situation of each nonprofit organization; it can be expanded to include other federal or state lobbying compliance issues.

Compliance Policy

A. Model Employee Letter

Dear Colleague:

As a registrant under the Lobbying Disclosure Act ("LDA"), [insert Nonprofit Organization Name here ("ABC")] is regulated by a myriad of strict federal lobbying and ethics laws. The LDA, as amended in 2007, prohibits all gifts, travel reimbursement, or honoraria to Members and employees of the U.S. Congress from lobbyists, foreign agents, and their employers, such as ABC. Criminal penalties and stiff civil penalties apply to those who violate the law.

As a lobbyist employer, ABC must certify to the Clerk of the House and the Secretary of the Senate on a semi-annual basis that our organization has not made an illegal gift, travel reimbursement, or honoraria to a Member or employee of Congress. Even a non-lobbyist employee of ABC can cause our organization to violate the law simply where that non-lobbyist employee makes a payment on behalf of a member or employee of Congress using ABC-reimbursed funds.

ABC has a "no-gift/travel/honorarium" policy that prohibits gifts, travel, or honoraria for any specified federal government official. In effect, no ABC funds, property, use of facilities, or services of any kind may be given to, or used for the benefit of, any Member or employee of the U.S. Congress. Under certain circumstances, prior written approval may be given for certain payments, travel, or events if cleared by the [insert CEO, General Counsel, or another appropriate individual].

Attached is a Fact Sheet detailing some specifics of these laws.

Thank you for your assistance with this compliance.

If you have any questions, please contact:

Signature

B. Model Policy

POLICY ON GIFTS/TRAVEL/HONORARIA TO CONGRESSIONAL OFFICIALS

As an entity that employs federal lobbyists, ABC is subject to criminal and civil liability if it makes any illegal gifts, provides travel or travel reimbursement, or grants honoraria to a Member or employee of the U.S. Congress. Any employee of ABC can cause the organization to violate this law, even inadvertently, if, for example, the employee buys drinks or dinner for a Congressional official and obtains reimbursement from ABC.

ABC's policy prohibits the making of, or reimbursement for, any gifts, travel, or honoraria to Members or employees of Congress. This means that no ABC money, property, use of facilities, or services of any kind may be given or used for the benefit of Congressional officials whether in the form of gifts, travel, travel reimbursement, honoraria, or similar assistance. Under certain circumstances prior written approval may be given for certain payments, travel, or events if cleared by [insert CEO, General Counsel, or another appropriate individual].

"Gifts" are defined broadly to include, among other things, meals, tickets to sporting and entertainment events, invitations to receptions, books, baseball caps and T-shirts, trinkets, free use of [Nonprofit Organization's] facilities and equipment, airline or train tickets, hotel or resort stays, golf or tennis fees, and use of a car service.

"Congressional official" includes anyone who is a U.S. Senator, a U.S. Representative, or who is employed by the U.S. Congress. It also includes a

Congressional official interviewing with ABC for a job.

ABC has a "no tolerance" policy on gifts/travel/honoraria to Congressional officials. Noncompliance can result in discipline to employees, including termination. Questions about this ABC policy are to be addressed to [insert CEO, General Counsel, or another appropriate individual].

C. Model Internal "Attestation Letter"

GIFTS/TRAVEL/HONORARIA ATTESTATION

The Honest Leadership and Open Government Act of 2007 (the "Act"), signed by the President on September 14, 2007, amended provisions of the Lobbying Disclosure Act, as well as the gift provisions of the Rules of the House and of the Senate (the "Rules"). The amendments not only prohibit most gifts to Members and employees of the United States Congress, but also place the burden of compliance on the lobbyists and lobbyists' employers, which includes ABC. Thus, the act of giving illegal gifts, travel, or honoraria to Members and employees of Congress by ABC is subject to civil and criminal penalties.

I recognize that, as a result of these restrictions, ABC must file a certification statement on a semi-annual basis. This statement must certify that ABC has read and understands the gift/travel/honoraria provisions of the Rules, and has not provided, directed, or requested the providing of a gift, travel, or honoraria to a Member or employee of the U.S. Congress with knowledge that it would violate the Rules.

I certify and am familiar with the applicable provisions of the Rules.

For the period _____ [enter semi-annual period], I certify to the best of my knowledge that:

- ◆ I have exercised due diligence and am not aware of any unlawful gifts, travel, or honoraria for a Member or employee of the U.S. Congress made, incurred by, or reimbursed to any ABC employees; or

- ◆ The gifts/travel/honoraria described in the attached document were made or reimbursed by ABC.

_____
Print

_____
Signature

_____
Title

_____
Date

19B
Joint Venture Agreement

Note: Associations and other nonprofit organizations are increasingly enter-ing into joint venture agreements or other similar contract arrangements with commercial businesses. For some kinds of endeavors that provide pro-grams or services to an organization's membership or other constituencies, the conventional approach of sponsoring or endorsing the offerings of a commercial firm are suitable, such as has long been common with credit card programs, insurance programs, and so on. There the exempt organ-ization must remain almost completely "passive" to the program or serv-ice to avoid unrelated business income tax ("UBIT") on the royalties typically received by the organization (although a side agreement for active management or marketing, generating UBIT-eligible income for the organ-ization, is also common). But if the association or other exempt organiza-tion desires to have ownership interest and active participation in the program or service, another approach is appropriate. The organization can "partner" with the commercial business in a joint venture (although the terms "partner" and "partnership" have distinct, and often unintended, legal consequences and should be avoided). In a joint venture, which is a contract relationship, the exempt organization and the taxable business together own and operate the program or service. Usually there is no tax-ation at the joint venture level; instead, each joint venture participant realizes income or loss according to its own tax situation. For the exempt organization, if the endeavors of the joint venture are consistent with its exempt purposes and the arrangement is structured appropriately, this can often mean that its share of net income is tax exempt. Note that there are specific and non-intuitive Internal Revenue Service pronouncements on joint ventures and other similar arrangements involving exempt organi-zations; and the annual informational tax return Form 990 (2008) requires disclosure to the IRS and to the public about these relationships. Expert legal and tax advice is essential before entering into them.

Agreement

This Agreement ("Agreement") is entered into as of _____, 20__, be-tween _____, a tax-exempt nonprofit corporation headquartered at _____ ("ABC"), and _____, a taxable equity corporation headquar-tered at _____ ("XYZ") for mutual consideration, the receipt and ade-quacy of which are acknowledged by the parties, who agree:

1. <u>Nature of the Joint Venture.</u> Through this Agreement, ABC and XYZ are together developing, launching, marketing, and managing an endeavor to provide _____ services to the constituencies of ABC using the reputa-tions, resources, relationships, finances, media channels, expertise, and

experience of both ABC and XYZ. ABC and XYZ will each use its best efforts to make this a successful and long-standing joint venture relationship. Each represents and acknowledges that it does not have undisclosed conflicts of interest – competing business relationships elsewhere — that would impair its ability to fulfill its duties under this Agreement aggressively and completely.

2. <u>Relationship to ABC's Tax Exemption.</u> The _____ services that are the subject of this endeavor are, and will throughout the term of this Agreement remain, consistent with the purposes for which ABC has been determined by the Internal Revenue Service (IRS) to be exempt from federal income tax. The _____ services are described in Attachment A to this Agreement. No other services, endeavors, activities, or arrangements will be the subject of this Agreement. If during the term of this Agreement there are court decisions, IRS pronouncements or other legal or tax changes or developments that might affect the _____ services that are the subject of this Agreement as being consistent with ABC's federal income tax exemption, the parties will amend the Agreement accordingly or terminate it.

3. <u>Name.</u> The endeavor operates under the name _____, with the acronym _____, with the name and acronym registered to the extent feasible at the U.S. Department of Commerce Patent and Trademark Office. These and any other marks uniquely attributable to the endeavor are owned by ABC and XYZ in proportion to their respective ownership shares in the endeavor.

4. <u>Ownership Interests.</u> ABC will have a fifty-one percent (51%) ownership interest, and XYZ will have a forty-nine percent (49%) ownership interest, in all property and assets, tangible or intangible, that are created, developed, purchased, or otherwise owned, obtained, earned, or accrued under this Agreement other than as provided by its terms, specifically excluding any interests of ABC, XYZ, or a third party that are licensed to the endeavor or are otherwise acquired or obtained partially, temporarily, or conditionally, in which case the terms of those licenses or other relationships will prevail. *Alternative: ABC will have a fifty percent (50%) ownership interest and XYZ will have a fifty percent (50%) ownership interest in all property . . . ABC will, however, have sole and exclusive authority for all management and decision making concerning those aspects of the endeavor that relate to ABC's federal income tax exempt purposes, specifically _____.*

5. <u>Management Committee.</u> The endeavor is managed by a Management Committee, which will have exclusive authority and responsibility for managing the endeavor consistent with this Agreement. The Management Committee consists of six (6) members, three (3) appointed by each ABC and XYZ. The Committee will have a Chairman elected by the Committee, with the Chairman position alternating annually between a representative of ABC and of XYZ. The terms of the members of the Management Committee will have no limits. The Committee will deliberate and vote by majority. A

quorum for Committee decision making is a majority of Committee members. Meetings will be held in person or by telephone conference call when called by the Chairman with reasonable notice to Committee members. ABC and XYZ will each indemnify, and provide liability insurance for, its appointees on the Management Committee. Members of the Management Committee may be reimbursed for their expenses incurred directly from performance of their duties on the Management Committee and, if approved by ABC and XYZ, may be paid reasonable stipends for their service on the Management Committee. The Management Committee may appoint other committees that, in the Committee's discretion, are necessary or desirable for management of the endeavor, with membership on those other committees consisting of members of the Management Committee or others. The Management Committee will have the authority to engage consultants at reasonable rates to assist in any aspect of the endeavor or in the Committee's work. The endeavor will not have its own employees unless recommended by the Management Committee and approved by both ABC and XYZ.

6. <u>Capitalization.</u> ABC and XYZ will each provide initial capitalization to the endeavor, with the relative value of the capitalization provided by each party consistent with its respective proportional ownership interest. The initial capitalization provided by each party will be deemed and considered for all purposes to be adequate and equitable. Capitalization may be in the form of cash or valuable tangible or intangible property. Additional capitalization in the form of "cash calls" or otherwise may be required of ABC and XYZ during the operations of the endeavor as recommended by the Management Committee and approved by both ABC and XYZ. The initial capitalization provided by ABC and XYZ is described in Attachment B to this Agreement.

7. <u>Distributions.</u> At the conclusion of each fiscal year of the Agreement, the Management Committee will determine what if any amount of net return achieved by the endeavor to retain for operating capital and what if any amount of net return to be distributed to the parties proportionately according to their ownership shares. The decisions of the Management Committee are in the Committee's sole and exclusive discretion.

8. <u>Accounting and Audit.</u> This endeavor of ABC and XYZ will follow accounting and tax requirements for a partnership unless otherwise recommended by the Management Committee and approved by both ABC and XYZ. An annual audit will be prepared under the direction of the Management Committee and furnished to ABC and XYZ. ABC and XYZ will each have the right upon reasonable notice to review or audit the books and records of the endeavor, including through the use of outside consultants to either party.

9. <u>Licenses.</u> ABC and XYZ each provide a non-exclusive license for use in the endeavor of the name, acronym, and logo of each, and any other marks, copyrights, lists, or other intellectual property of each used in the endeavor, with the license limited to use to advance and improve the endeavor and not for other purposes, and with each type of use subject to

written approval in advance by the party whose intellectual property is to be used. Upon termination of the Agreement for any reason, this license is cancelled and all use of the intellectual property will cease.

10. Confidentiality. ABC and XYZ will each have access during the term of this Agreement to confidential information of the other, including confidential business or other information. Confidential information will include, but not be limited to, that which is marked "confidential" or that which either party should reasonably expect that the other party would intend to maintain as confidential. Each party will respect and treat this confidential information of the other party in the same way, and using the same procedures, that it respects and treats its own most confidential information. Neither party will disclose any of this confidential without the written approval of its owner except under compulsion of law.

11. Other Parties. Other parties may participate in this endeavor upon the terms and conditions that are recommended by the Management Committee and approved by both ABC and XYZ. Other parties will be subject to at least the terms and conditions of this Agreement.

12. Obligations of ABC. ABC will have those obligations in connection with the endeavor as are described in Attachment C.i.

13. Obligations of XYZ. XYZ will have those obligations in connection with the endeavor as are described in Attachment C.ii.

14. Term and Termination without Cause. This Agreement is effective upon its execution by ABC and XYZ. The Agreement is for a five-year (5-year) term and is automatically renewed for additional five-year (5-year) terms on each fifth (5th) anniversary of the Agreement unless either ABC or XYZ provides written notice of termination without cause at least one (1) year prior to a five-year (5-year) anniversary of the Agreement.

15. Termination with Cause. Upon the breach of this Agreement by either party, the other party may give ninety-day (90-day) notice, stating in detail the alleged breach, and opportunity for the other party to cure the breach. If the other party fails to cure the breach within that ninety-day (90-day) period, the Agreement is terminated for cause.

16. Effect of Termination. Upon the effective date of termination of this Agreement with or without cause, all of the obligations and responsibilities of ABC and XYZ under this Agreement will cease, except for the obligation to maintain the confidentiality of the other party's confidential information. All property and assets, tangible or intangible, that are created, developed, purchased, or otherwise owned, obtained, earned, or accrued under this Agreement will be divided between the parties in proportion to their ownership shares. For those items which cannot be readily divided, such as intellectual property, they will be offered to third parties or, at the written request of either ABC or XYZ, an auction process developed and operated by a third party acceptable to both ABC and XYZ will be conducted to offer and sell the property to either ABC or XYZ, whichever is the highest bidder,

with the proceeds of the auction, less expenses, divided between the parties in proportion to their ownership shares.

17. <u>Dispute Resolution.</u> Any dispute or disagreement arising in any way under or in connection with this Agreement, the decisions of the Management Committee or of the parties, or otherwise will be resolved by binding arbitration in which each party will select a nominator and the two nominators will select a single arbitrator, with the arbitrator instructed to resolve the dispute as quickly and efficiently as possible, ideally with no or only the most minimal discovery, and with the arbitrator establishing the procedures and making any award, including injunctive relief, that the arbitrator deems just and reasonable and with both parties agreeing to abide by the award of the arbitrator and making no appeal in any forum from that award.

18. <u>Amendments.</u> This Agreement contains the entire agreement and understanding of the parties with respect to the subject matter of the Agreement. No other agreements or understandings of the parties with respect to the subject matter are valid or enforceable, nor will be considered in interpreting or enforcing this Agreement. Any changes to this Agreement require the recommendation of the Management Committee and the written approval of both ABC and XYZ.

19. <u>Relationship.</u> ABC and XYZ expressly acknowledge and warrant that they are, and will remain, separate legal entities. The relationship between ABC and XYZ is exclusively as provided in this Agreement. No other agency, partnership, or joint venture arrangement is intended except as provided in this Agreement. Neither party is authorized to incur any liability, obligation, or expense on behalf of the other except under the terms of this Agreement.

20. <u>Indemnification.</u> ABC and XYZ each indemnify and will hold harmless the other party, its officers, directors, agents, members, shareholders, employees, and appointees to the Management Committee from and against any action, suit, proceeding, claim, damage, liability, obligation, cost or expense that may arise by reason of any act or omission by the indemnifying party, its officers, directors, agents, members, shareholders, employees, and appointees to the Management Committee. The indemnification will include any settlement, damages, or legal defense costs reasonably incurred by the indemnified party.

21. <u>Notices.</u> Any notices or communications required under this Agreement will be in writing and will become effective five (5) days after mailing, postage prepaid, addressed to the current President or chief executive officer of the recipient party.

22. <u>Authority.</u> ABC and XYZ each represents and warrants that the individual who executes this Agreement on the part of that party has the full and unfettered legal authority to do so and, upon execution, the Agreement will become the obligation and responsibility of the party.

23. <u>Assignment.</u> This Agreement may be assigned only upon the prior written approval of the other party.

24. <u>Effect of Merger, Consolidation, or Bankruptcy.</u> In the event of merger, consolidation, or bankruptcy of ABC or XYZ, this Agreement will be considered terminated for cause.

25. <u>Counterparts.</u> This Agreement may be signed in counterparts.

26. <u>Governing Law.</u> This Agreement is governed by the law of the State of _____.

ABC   XYZ

By _____   By _____

Name _____   Name _____

Title _____   Title _____

Date _____   Date _____

Attachment A

Describe in detail the services to be provided pursuant to the Joint Venture Agreement.

Attachment B

Describe the initial capitalization provided by ABC and by XYZ.

Attachment C

C.i. Describe the obligations of ABC.
C.ii. Describe the obligations of XYZ.

20A
Agreement for Cost Sharing with Affiliate

Note: A cost-sharing agreement between a main association or other non-profit tax-exempt organization and its co-managed affiliate, subsidiary, foundation, chapter, or other nonprofit tax-exempt or for-profit taxable organization is often recommended in order to properly allocate expenses and avoid unrelated business income tax to the main association for revenues that might otherwise be characterized as "management fees." This agreement formalizes the co-management arrangement by confirming the separateness of the organizations to help protect the tax exemption status of the main association (as well as that of the other organization if it has tax exemption in a different category) and to help protect both organizations against liability that might arise from tort or contract claims if there were an attempt to "pierce the corporate veil."

Agreement

This Agreement ("Agreement") is entered into as of _____ _____, 20__, between _____ (the "Association") and _____ (the "Affiliate") for mutual consideration, the receipt and adequacy of which are acknowledged by the parties, who agree:

1. Purpose. The Association approves of the mission, purpose, and activities of the Affiliate and has agreed that the Affiliate may share use of certain of the Association's office space, business equipment and supplies, administrative services (i.e., human resources, accounting, information technology, etc.), and staff time on a cost-sharing basis as described in this Agreement. The Affiliate represents and warrants that it will conduct all activities in accordance with all applicable laws and regulations.

2. Cost Sharing. The Association and the Affiliate will share costs as follows:

a. The Affiliate will utilize and reimburse for those facilities or services, which may include office space, business equipment and supplies, administrative services, and staff time, as itemized by category and described in detail in Attachment A to this Agreement.

b. The Affiliate will reimburse the Association on a monthly basis for the Affiliate's share of the costs incurred by the Association in providing the facilities and services on Attachment A including a ___-percent fee to reimburse the Association for its general and administrative expenses in sharing the facilities and services to the Affiliate.

3. Books and Records. All books, records, documents, copyrights, trademarks, and other material prepared for the Affiliate by the Association, and any intangible or other property paid for by the Affiliate, will be assigned,

transferred, and belong exclusively to the Affiliate. The Affiliate will have the right to inspect and/or remove all of its tangible or intangible property at any time with reasonable notice to the Association subject to the termination provisions of this Agreement. The Association will provide to the Affiliate copies of books, records, time sheets, and accounts relevant to this Agreement upon request.

4. Other Activities. The Affiliate acknowledges that the Association is engaged in other activities on behalf of the Association's mission and constituency and that the Association's employees and agents will be performing other services than those referenced in this Agreement. However, the Association will not, without the Affiliate's prior written consent, undertake to perform any services for any person, firm, corporation, or other organization that would create a conflict between the duties of the Association to the Affiliate and those to that other person or organization.

5. Evaluation. The governing board of the Affiliate or any body delegated by that governing board will annually review with the Association the working relationship between the Association and the Affiliate. A written evaluation shall be given to the Association each year upon request.

6. Termination. This Agreement may be amended or terminated at any time by the mutual written agreement of the Association and the Affiliate. This Agreement will terminate upon written notice of one party to the other upon any of the following events: (a) the bankruptcy or dissolution of the Association or the Affiliate; (b) ninety (90) days after the sending of a written notice of an intention to terminate this Agreement by either the Association or the Affiliate to the other party; (c) upon the material breach of this Agreement, following written notice to the breaching party, opportunity by the breaching party to cure the material breach within thirty (30) days, and failure of the breaching party to cure the material breach; or (d) immediately upon fraudulent or criminal acts by either party. Upon termination by either party for any reason: all records, files, materials, correspondence, other property and related items belonging to the Affiliate will promptly be shipped or otherwise delivered to such person or place as the Affiliate designates in writing.

7. Relationship. The Association's relationship with the Affiliate in the performance of this Agreement is based on cost sharing, and no agency, partnership, or joint venture arrangement is intended. All employees or agents performing services that are to be performed by the Association under this Agreement will at all times be under the Association's exclusive direction and control and shall be employees or agents of the Association and not of the Affiliate.

8. Confidentiality. The Association and its employees will use best efforts, during the term of this Agreement or at any time after termination of this Agreement, to avoid disclosure of any confidential information acquired by the Association in the performance of services under this Agreement, except as permitted in writing by the Affiliate or required under compulsion of law.

9. Notices. Any notices or communications required under this Agreement will be in writing and will become effective five (5) days after mailing, postage prepaid, addressed to the current Chairman/President of the recipient party.

10. Assignment. This Agreement may be assigned only upon the prior written approval of the other party.

11. Waiver. Waiver by either party of any term or condition of this Agreement, or any breach of the Agreement, will not constitute a waiver of any other term or condition.

12. Effect of Agreement. This Agreement is binding upon, and will inure to the benefit of, the parties to this Agreement and their respective successors and assigns. This Agreement contains all of the terms agreed upon by the parties with respect to the subject matter of this Agreement and supersedes all prior agreements, arrangements, and communications between the parties concerning the subject matter, whether oral or written.

13. Governing Law. This Agreement will be governed by the laws of the State of _____.

(Association)

By: _____

Title: _____

Date: _____

(Affiliate)

By: _____

Title: _____

Date: _____

_____

Attachment A

[Include in Attachment A, by categories and itemized with as much description as possible, all office space, business equipment and supplies, administrative services (i.e., human resources, accounting, information technology, etc.), and staff time that is subject to the Agreement.]

20B
Agreement with Chapter

Note: Many national, regional, or other central associations have arrangements with chapters or affiliates, with the "subordinate organizations" (the term used by the Internal Revenue Service for group federal income tax exemption) often organized on a geographic basis but potentially organized on other bases such as subject interest. The essence of any such arrangement is the central organization offering the opportunity for the chapter to associate with, and use the name of, the central organization in return for the chapter offering to abide by the rules of the collective body, often called a "federation." Key features of the arrangement are the grant of a charter, license of use of a common denomination, conformity with basic rules for chapters, and termination features. This sample or model is a very basic version of an agreement with, or charter for, a chapter or affiliate.

Agreement

This Agreement ("Agreement") is entered into as of _____ _____, 20__, between _____ (the "Association") and _____ (the "Chapter") for mutual consideration, the receipt and adequacy of which are acknowledged by the parties, who agree:

1. Grant of Charter. The Association grants a non-exclusive charter to the Chapter to be an affiliated chapter of the Association, with the Chapter authorized to use the designation "__ (State)__ _____Association, Chapter of the National _____ Association," and with authority to use this designation, or any appropriate contraction or acronym of it, in connection with the policies, programs, activities, and events of the Chapter as authorized in this Agreement and subject to the terms and conditions of the Agreement. The Chapter will serve the constituency of the Association in the geographic area of _____. This grant of a charter by the Association to the Chapter includes a limited right to use certain intellectual property of the Association, such as its trademarks or copyrights, subject to the terms and conditions in this Agreement.

2. Membership. All members of the Chapter also must maintain active membership in the Association in accordance with the provisions, procedures, and applicable due schedules of the Association. The Chapter will deny the application of, or terminate the membership of, any person or firm that does not maintain membership in the Association and inform the Association in writing of its intention to do so.

3. Obligations of the Association. The Association's obligations to the chapter include the following:

a. Education Programs. The Association will assist the Chapter in developing, marketing, and presenting educational programs in a variety of formats in the Chapter's geographic area or via the Chapter's Web site, with that education tailored where practicable to the specific needs of the constituency of the Chapter.

b. Financial Management Assistance. The Association will assist the Chapter with the collection, accounting, and disbursing of Chapter funds. The Association will collect Chapter dues from members of the Chapter and promptly transmit the dues receipts to the Chapter. The Chapter will be eligible to participate in the group federal income tax exemption obtained and managed by the Association subject to Internal Revenue Service and Association requirements and obligations for that group exemption.

c. Representation. The Chapter will nominate __ individuals to serve on the Council of Chapter Representatives managed by the Association and convening at the annual meeting and other meetings of the Association.

d. Marketing and Communications. The Association will assist the Chapter in promoting membership, in marketing members' participation at programs and attendance at meetings, and in preparing newsletter and other communications from the Chapter to its constituency.

4. Obligations of the Chapter. The Chapter's obligations to the Association include the following:

a. Structure. The Chapter will remain incorporated as a nonprofit corporation under the laws of its state and will maintain federal income tax exemption either as part of the Association's group exemption program or otherwise. The articles of incorporation or corporate charter of the Chapter, and its bylaws, will be consistent with those of the Association. Any changes to either document of the Chapter are subject to advance written approval by the Association.

b. Purposes and Activities. The Chapter will conduct all of its policies, programs, activities, and events in accordance with applicable legal and regulatory provisions and using the highest ethical standards.

c. Liability. The Chapter will refrain from representing, and will use best efforts to compel representatives of the Chapter to refrain from representing, that any policies, programs, activities, events, statements, positions, communications, or representations emanate from, or are endorsed by, the Association unless specifically permitted in writing by the Association. The Chapter will maintain liability insurance with coverage and limits acceptable to the Association.

d. Educational Programs. The Chapter will sponsor and promote educational and other programs of the Association and will use its best efforts to ensure that educational programs of the Chapter are of the highest quality with respect to program content, materials, and logistical preparation.

5. Intellectual Property. The Chapter will not use, or cause, or permit to be used by any person, any logos, trademark, service marks, or copyrighted materials of the Association without Association's prior written consent, other than the limited use of that intellectual property in connection with performance of the specific obligations of the Chapter provided in this Agreement. The Chapter will ensure that the applicable copyright or trademark notice is used with any Association intellectual property as appropriate. Upon the expiration or termination of this Agreement, all use by the Chapter of the Association's intellectual property will end immediately. The Chapter's obligations to protect the Association's intellectual property will survive the expiration or termination of this Agreement.

6. Revocation or Surrender of the Charter. The charter granted to the Chapter by this Agreement, with all of its attendant rights and obligations, will remain in full force and effect until and unless revoked by the Association or surrendered by the Chapter in accordance with the following provisions.

a. Revocation. The Association, through its Board of Directors, has the right and authority to revoke the Chapter's charter if the Board determines that the conduct of the Chapter is in violation of this Agreement or the provisions of the Association's bylaws or applicable policies or procedures. Any decision by the Association to revoke the Chapter's charter will be initiated by written notice to the Chapter specifying the reasons for the revocation, with the Chapter provided the opportunity to respond to the Association's Board of Directors in writing or, if permitted by the Board, in person. The decision of the Board is final; and the Chapter specifically warrants that it will assert no appeal to that decision in any other forum.

b. Surrender. The Chapter may surrender its charter by delivering notice of its intention to do so at least sixty (60) days in advance of the effective date of the surrender to the Board of Directors of the Association.

c. The Association's Rights after Revocation or Surrender. After revocation or surrender of the Chapter's charter, the Association will have the right to notify each member of the Chapter of the fact of the revocation or surrender and will have the sole authority to organize a new Chapter of those members to replace the former Chapter of the Association. The Chapter will cease to represent or suggest any affiliation with the Association and will return any Association property or assets that may be in the possession of the Chapter at the time of revocation or surrender of the charter.

7. Relationship. The Association and the Chapter expressly acknowledge and warrant that they are, and will remain, separate legal entities. The Association's relationship with the Chapter in the performance of this Agreement is based on a charter, and no agency, partnership, or joint venture arrangement is intended. Neither party is authorized to incur any liability, obligation, or expense on behalf of the other. Each party will indemnify and hold harmless the other party, its officers, directors, agents, members, and employees, from and against any action, suit, proceeding,

claim, damage, liability, obligation, cost, or expense that may arise by reason of any act or omission by the party, its officers, directors, or agents. All employees or agents performing services that are to be performed by the Association under this Agreement will at all times be under the Association's exclusive direction and control and will be employees or agents of the Association and not of the Chapter. All employees or agents performing services that are to be performed by the Chapter under this Agreement will at all times be under the Chapter's exclusive direction and control and will be employees or agents of the Chapter and not of the Association.

8. Confidentiality. The Association and the Chapter may at times come into possession of confidential information of the other. That confidential information will be maintained in confidence and will be subjected to the same level of protection that each party would utilize for its own similar confidential information. Neither the Association nor the Chapter will disclose confidential information of the other except as permitted in writing by the other or required under compulsion of law.

9. Notices. Any notices or communications required under this Agreement will be in writing and will become effective five (5) days after mailing, postage prepaid, addressed to the current Chairman/President of the recipient party.

10. Assignment. This Agreement may be assigned only upon the prior written approval of the other party.

CHAPTER   ASSOCIATION

By _____   By _____

Name _____   Name _____

Title _____   Title _____

Date _____   Date _____

Updated Document

11
Records Retention Policy

Note: All nonprofit organizations and associations know the value of prudent records maintenance. It is increasingly clear that periodic purging of unused paper and electronic documents can pay major dividends to an organization: reduced storage costs, reduced costs of search and production when documents are sought in litigation or government investigations from the organization as a third party, and greater ease in locating those documents that are retained and not purged. This is a relatively straightforward records retention policy for a nonprofit organization. Note that the keys to successful implementation of a policy such as this are top-down commitment and organization-wide compliance.

Records Retention

Principal Rules

Rule 1. Paper and electronic documents that are indicated below as falling within Categories A, B, C or D are to be transferred to and maintained by the Human Resources Department, Legal Department, or Administrative Department (or their equivalents).

Rule 2. Other paper documents, wherever located, are to be discarded every three years.

Rule 3. Other electronic documents are to be deleted annually from all individual personnel computer memories, from all organization networks, and from all backups.

Rule 4. Copies of paper or electronic records may be retained individually by appropriate staff members for historical or ongoing work reasons but only upon the written approval of _____.

Rule 5. No paper or electronic records are to be destroyed or deleted if pertinent to an anticipated or ongoing government investigation or proceeding or to any anticipated or ongoing private litigation.

Category A: Retain Permanently

Governance Records: Articles of Incorporation (or equivalent), Bylaws, other organizational documents, governing board and committee minutes.
Maintained by Legal.

Tax Records: Filed state and federal tax reports and returns, tax exemption determination letter and related correspondence, files related to tax audits, and supporting information and documentation for federal and state returns, deductions, refunds, and similar uses
Maintained by Administrative.

Intellectual Property Records: Copyright and trademark registrations and samples of protected works.
Maintained by Legal.

Financial Records: Audited financial statements, attorney contingent liability letters.
Maintained by Administrative.

Category B: Retain for 10 Years

Pension and Benefit Records: Pension (ERISA) plan participant/beneficiary records, actuarial reports, related correspondence with government agencies, and supporting records.
Maintained by Human Resources.

Lobbying Records: State and federal lobbying registration and reporting documents and back-up information.
Maintained by Legal.

Category C: Retain for Three Years

Employee/Employment Records: Employee names, addresses, Social Security numbers, dates of birth, INS Forms I-9, resume/application materials, job descriptions, dates of hire and termination/separation, evaluations, compensation information, promotions, transfers, disciplinary matters, time/payroll records, leave/comp time/FMLA, engagement and discharge correspondence, and documentation of basis for independent contractor status (retain for all current employees and independent contractors and for three years after departure of each individual).
Maintained by Human Resources.

Lease, Insurance, and Contract/License Records: Software license agreements; vendor, hotel, and service agreements; independent contractor agreements; employment agreements; consultant agreements; and all other agreements (retain during the term of the agreement and for three years after the termination, expiration, or nonrenewal of each agreement).
Maintained by Legal.

Category D: Retain for One Year

All Other Paper or Electronic Records: Correspondence files, past budgets, bank statements, publications, employee manuals/policies and procedures, and survey information.
Maintained by relevant department.

Association Law Handbook, Fourth Edition 2009 Supplement Additions to the Fourth Edition

1. Chapter 9, **Sarbanes-Oxley Governance Reforms**, Page 29
Insert in **Chapter 9 Resources** under "Articles":

> Brody. "The Board of Nonprofit Organizations: Puzzling through the Gaps between Law and Practice." *Fordham Law Review* 76 (2007): 521.

2. Chapter 11, **Personal Liability of Officers & Directors**, Page 43
Insert in **Chapter 11 Resources** under a new heading "Articles":

> Jacobs. "Your Legal Responsibilities: Key Duties and Key Laws That All Board Members Should Know." *Associations Now* (January 2008): 70.

3. Chapter 18, **Chief Executive Employment Contract**, Page 82
Insert in *Chapter 18 Resources* under "Cases":

> *People v. Grasso*, 861 N.Y.S.2d 627 (N.Y. App. Div. 2008). Court denial of State of New York proceeding against CEO of New York Stock Exchange ("NYSE") for allegedly receiving excessive severance compensation from not-for-profit corporation.

Insert in **Chapter 18 Resources** under "Articles":

> McDowell. "Compensation and Expense Reimbursement for Association Executives." *Association Law & Policy* (October 10, 2007): 1.

4. Chapter 22, **Mergers & Consolidations**, Page 100
Insert in **Chapter 22 Resources** under a new heading "Articles":

> Jacobs. "Mergers: Easier (and Harder) Than You Think." *Associations Now* (July 2008): 33.

5. Chapter 23, **Legal Audit/Merger or Consolidation Due Diligence Review**, Page 106
Insert in **Chapter 23 Resources** under a new heading "Articles":

> Jacobs. "Mergers: Easier (and Harder) Than You Think." *Associations Now* (July 2008): 33.

6. Chapter 52, **Membership Restrictions**, Page 246
Insert in **Chapter 52 Resources** under "Books":

> ABA Section of Antitrust Law. *Antitrust and Associations Handbook* (2009).

7. Chapter 55, **Membership Services to Nonmembers**, Page 262
Insert in **Chapter 55 Resources** under "Books":

ABA Section of Antitrust Law. *Antitrust and Associations Handbook* (2009).

8. Chapter 56, **Business or Professional Codes of Ethics & Self-Regulation**, Page 267
Insert in **Chapter 56 Resources** under "Books":

ABA Section of Antitrust Law. *Antitrust and Associations Handbook* (2009).

9. Chapter 57, **Statistical Surveys**, Page 275
Insert in **Chapter 57 Resources** under "Books":

ABA Section of Antitrust Law. *Antitrust and Associations Handbook* (2009).

10. Chapter 60, **Standards Development**, Page 291
Insert in **Chapter 60 Resources** under "Books":

ABA Section of Antitrust Law. *Antitrust and Associations Handbook* (2009).

Insert in **Chapter 60 Resources** under "Cases" at the end of *In Re Rambus*:

On appeal to the Federal Appellate Court, the court reversed the Commission decision, finding inadequate evidence of anticompetitive intent and conduct. 522 F.3d 456 (D.C. Cir. 2008), *cert. denied*, __ U.S. __, 77. U.S.L.W. 3346 (2009).

Broadcom Corp. v. Qualcomm Inc., 501 F.3d 297 (3d Cir. 2007). Litigation over violation by standards development participant of its commitment to provide reasonable and nondiscriminatory ("RAND") terms for licensing of patents embedded in standards.

11. Chapter 70, **Antitrust & Lobbying**, Page 348
Insert in **Chapter 70 Resources** under "Books":

ABA Section of Antitrust Law. *Antitrust and Associations Handbook* (2009).

12. Chapter 72, **Antitrust Enforcement**, Page 356
Insert in **Chapter 72 Resources** under"Books":

ABA Section of Antitrust Law, *Antitrust and Associations Handbook* (2009).

13. Chapter 84, **Non-Deductibility of Dues Because of Lobbying**, Page 429
Change the reference "IRC Section 603(e)" to a corrected reference:

IRC Section 6033(e)

INDEX

Note: A page number followed by an "n" and another number refers to a note on the designated page. For example, 101n1 refers to note 1 on page 101.